Interpersonal Communication

How to Communicate Effectively, Build Great Relationships, and Relate to Others

By: Discover Press

Table of Contents

Introduction

What comes to mind when the word "communication" arises? Speaking? Text messaging? Sign language? Maybe even nonverbal cues? In all reality, it would not take much to argue that communication as a concept is virtually limitless when considering all the different things that communicate, the information that can be communicated, and all the methods utilized to do so. Communication is so vast that it is customizable and used to express so much more than basic information. It even goes to the point of people having their own preferences and tastes over all of these methods of expression.

So, what is communication? How can this infinitely overwhelming concept be summarized into one blanket statement? For the sake of this book, the term "communication" will be operationally defined as the transference of information from one entity to another. Think about how this definition works alongside the images and associations that came to mind from the opening sentence. Does it fit? Does that pointless conversation you had on the phone with your friend qualify as communication? Does the businesswoman nonverbally shaking hands with her new hire count as communication? Is The Weeknd communicating with his audience when he sings "Blinding Lights" for the umpteenth time? In short, yes. However, the key to proper communication is context. "Communication" is a term that is often used generically—which is ironic because it is extremely powerful—not caring whether or not someone is willing to take advantage of it. Furthermore, it will very easily get past anyone who takes it for granted.

Consider this common stereotypical question within the study of philosophy: If a tree falls in a forest, and there is no one within miles to hear it, does it even produce a sound? Based on what is known about sound waves, it is safe to assume that yes, indeed, it does make a sound. Nevertheless, this continues to dominate many philosophical conversations and debates, as the rules of this question explicitly establish that there is no one around to confirm or deny this.

Now think about how this scenario applies to the operational definition of "communication." The term is defined for the sake of this book as one person or thing transferring information to another person or thing. According to this definition, there has to be at least one party on the transferring end, as well as one on the receiving end. With that established, is it not safe to say that communication cannot occur if no one is there to receive the information? Can someone say that they have effectively communicated if they upload videos on their YouTube channel, yet not a single video has one view?

Our current society has a concerning tendency to demote formalized forms of communication, deeming proper vocabulary as irrelevant and insufficient and having absolutely no place in popular culture. A text message with proper punctuation is often interpreted as stiff and annoying. It can even be viewed as aggressive in some cases. Similarly, professional settings discourage causality in verbal interactions, writing, attire, and even the way you pretend to laugh at your boss's terrible jokes. Breaking away from the well-established template can very easily result in being terminated from a position. Again, all of this goes back to context.

The thought of having to switch your behavior and appearance on a whim can be intimidating, maybe seeming disingenuous and an insincere way of life. Although completely understandable, one of the goals of this book is to explain why this is not the case. One can act formally and still stay true to themself.

Now that I have your attention and, more importantly, have you thinking a little more about communication, let us narrow these bigger concepts down into the central focus of this book. As you have probably gathered from the very title of this book, we will be looking at interpersonal communication. The most basic characteristic that distinguishes interpersonal communication from our own operational definition of communication is that it is distinctly between humans. As such, the concept utilizes the means of communication that separate us from other creatures and entities.

What are those characteristics? What sets us apart from cheetahs stalking antelope in a pack? What is the difference between a construction crew erecting a steel building and a colony of ants collaborating with one another to construct a hill? How are the birds migrating south for the winter any different than the elderly people moving to Florida for retirement? It all comes down to simply being more intelligent than other creatures, as one word summarizes things: personality.

The methods in which human beings communicate go so far beyond simply being able to speak and verbalize. Rather, it is everything that occurs behind the words. Human beings utilize emotions and expression to communicate, as opposed to simply acting on instinct. We laugh, cry, scream, whisper, sing, and even alter our own voices in certain situations. Similarly, we utilize different means of verbal expression to convey said feelings. Humor is used in order to make people laugh or to diffuse an uncomfortable situation. Yelling and shouting is used to express the emotion of anger and the element of aggression. Additionally, our facial expressions also communicate emotions, many times without us even being completely cognizant that it is even occurring.

This last example of facial expressions, especially unconscious ones, serves as one of the main reasons that interpersonal communication is an art to be practiced. Have you ever found yourself in an unusual maybe even uncomfortable situation, and someone called you out on scowling? If so, hopefully it was of little to no consequence beyond some mild social embarrassment. However, imagine if you were in a staff meeting that you had been dreading for a while, and now that you are stuck in it, you are doing absolutely everything that you can to not fall asleep. The presenter lacks any and all personality, and the dry, dense material they are speaking about is delivered in the most monotone of voices. Outside of work, anyone could relate to getting sleepy during these. Nevertheless, any workplace expects people to listen and pay respect to the presenter or presenters.

Believe it or not, falling asleep during a meeting is a form of interpersonal communication. It is absolutely a means of expression. As you have probably already guessed, nodding off tells everyone around you that you are bored, unamused, and completely uninterested in whatever is going on. Many workplaces use the word "disengaged" as a negative criticism of such situations. These are the types of reputations that you want to avoid, regardless of the setting. Even with a couple of friends, you do not want to be known as "the one who never listens." It comes across as arrogant and makes people less likable without much turnaround time.

Social interactions can be complicated, without a single doubt. What's more is that they can be absolutely overwhelming to anyone who naturally struggles to adapt to different social environments. As such, this book adopted the simplest and most adaptable layout and approach. After all, one of the best pieces of advice to such an individual- one nervous to approach a social situation- is to err on the side of keeping things simple and uncomplicated.

The bulk of the book will take place in two main parts: "people" and "places." In other words, we will be breaking down some of the most important and essential components of interpersonal communication by putting them in the contexts in which they take place. To put it simply, start asking yourself two questions: "who do I socialize with, and where do I do it?" I can only imagine that your list is probably fairly long, so I have categorized some of the typical groups that you communicate with. Said people include family members, friends and acquaintances, significant others, co-workers, and the higher-ups in your company (i.e., bosses, directors, executives, etc.). These could include your direct boss or supervisor, directors, other supervisors, executives, and maybe even the very head of your company. This list may not be comprehensively applicable to your weekly encounters, as some groups that you encounter regularly have been left out. However, my objective in writing this book is to be specific enough with the groups that have been included that the information and scenarios presented here can apply to your other encounters as well.

In listing these groups of people, I am certain that you had your own mental associations when reading off the list. When seeing "significant other," you may have instantly thought about your spouse, dating partner, or that one special someone at the gym that you have been dying to ask out for the longest time. Maybe you are not even interested in having someone at this time in your life, and that is perfectly fine! When you read "co-workers," maybe your mind jumped to that drone of a co-worker that sits in the cubicle straight across from yours, with whom you always try to avoid eye contact in order to avoid setting off the ticking time bomb of pointless words that stream out. Perhaps with "family," your mind jumped to your great-aunt or -uncle, who you have not seen since you were seven-years-old, and you are nervous about visiting them in their retirement villa.

No matter who you associate these various roles with, you also likely associate particular locations with them. Skim over the previous paragraph. Each specific example featured a location: the gym, an adjacent cubicle, and a retirement villa. In addition to associating people with roles, or people with locations, our brains also tend to associate certain roles and relationships with different places. As such, the second section of this book will focus on typical locations and activities that require interpersonal communication at an essential level.

Examples will be presented sporadically throughout each category and each portion through the use of hypothetical scenarios. Additionally, I will add my own encounters with these concepts, regardless of whether or not I was successful in my own application of the concepts. These will be presented in the form of "Author's Experience" segments. Hopefully, you find these segments at the very least entertaining if not helpful. Nevertheless, I am sure we can all attest to having come out of our failures stronger, humbler, and more knowledgeable than we have through many of our successes.

Finally, before we get started, try to keep in mind that you might be the protagonist (a.k.a. main character) of your own story, though you are not a central character in the stories of everyone else that you encounter. Rather, you also fill in the blank as a member of one of the groups of people listed above and discussed in Part I. As such, there are two pieces of advice to be mindful of throughout our journey together. Firstly, go easy on others who may also struggle with communication. If someone makes a mistake that is not detrimental to your job or invasive in your life, do what you can to cut them some slack and ensure them that it is okay to make mistakes.

Secondly, try to be cognizant of your role in another's life, and communicate as someone in that role ought to. For instance, if you are the friend of someone who is going through a difficult time, do not view yourself solely as the protagonist of your own story line. Doing so will likely result in dismissing their needs and only considering how busy you are. Instead, take into consideration your role in their story as their friend. As the friend, you ought to do what you can to be there for them and provide support. Who knows, maybe they do not need your help at all and would simply appreciate you offering a listening ear. In any event, practice self-awareness and empathy (putting yourself in the metaphoric shoes of another and understanding what they are going through) as you consider the roles that you play in the lives of those around you.

With all of that in mind and said, let us move forward on this journey around interpersonal communication.

Part 1: People

Chapter 1: Family

There is a saying expressed and phrased differently depending on who is saying it. Essentially, it suggests that "nobody knows you better than yourself." There is so much truth to this proverb, as no one has the ability to know all of the "deep, dark" secrets that you have withheld from the world for years. As a wise star once said, "The inner machinations of my mind are an enigma."

In the same way that we are our own closest allies, no one knows your family like you do. Each and every family, no matter how dysfunctional or distant, has their own unique quirks and characteristics that set it aside from every other family. Perhaps the dysfunction is the very thing that defines it. In any case, only the members of your family are privy to those distinctions, and they are intertwined into all of us, whether we want them or not.

This is an important concept to note when discussing interpersonal communication. As we get to know ourselves and get in closer contact with the ways in which we communicate, we have to first consider what our parent(s) or guardian(s) taught us. Whether deliberate or not on the part of the parent or guardian, they have taught us so much simply by interacting with other people. As children, we learned so much through our eyes and ears by means of observation and, as a result, we all have at least a few of the same quirks as the people that raised us. Depending on said quirk, that can be anywhere on the spectrum of positive or negative, and its place on that spectrum is often subjectively based on belief and perspective.

Truman Capote's *Breakfast at Tiffany's* immediately comes to mind when discussing how we relate to our family. If you are not familiar with the book or the iconic film, it depicts the story of the fictitious Holly Golightly, who we later discover has run away from her upbringing as a simple, country girl, fleeing to New York and living a fraudulent life as a member of high society. Just as Holly's father catches up with her and tries to convince her to come home, our pasts will always find us in one way or another.

With this in mind, also consider the ways in which you communicate with your own immediate families. This does not mean your significant other or your children. Rather, think back on the people that raised you and anyone else you lived with: siblings, step-siblings, cousins, grandparents, aunts and uncles, etc. What rules of communication were established? Were those rules upheld or neglected? If you grew up with more than one parent or guardian, were the rules consistent between the two, or was one of them more lenient and let things slide on occasion?

The standards by which you are held is dependent on all of these factors and more. Take some time to try and objectively look at your home environment. Was it a place of order, chaos, or something in between? Pretend that you are a fly on the wall, maybe a security camera, looking at your family without any sense of bias or nostalgia. Obviously this is difficult, as you will always have some level of bias for or against your upbringing. Just pretend, or make your best effort to do so.

Imagine that you and any siblings you may have had are coming home from school after the average day of school. Nothing eventful occurred at school: no celebrations, no lamentations. You get off of the bus or get out of the car, or maybe you walk through the front door after walking home; what happens? Are you greeted with a smile, or yelled at from another room to keep it down? Do you throw your backpack on the floor and kick your shoes off to wherever they land, or do you put everything in a designated place? Does any type of conversation and interaction take place with another member of the household? Hugs? Kisses? Yelling or some form of negative physical contact?

Once you have settled in, where do you go? What do you do? Is it time for homework or television? Do you reach for a textbook or a video game controller? Maybe you run outside to play with the neighborhood friends until the streetlights come on. Have you still yet to encounter another member of the household? Perhaps they are still working, or perhaps no one in the household works. Do your activities include your sibling(s)? Did friends come over frequently, or did you yourself go and visit them often?

By the time the evening rolls around, what does bedtime look like? Are you expected to get in bed by a certain time, or is it a free-for-all? If your guardian tells you to start winding down and getting ready for bed, do you listen? What repercussions, if any, come as a result of disobeying this routine? How do you wish your family "goodnight"?

Okay, that was a lot of questions. I hope that this got you thinking a little bit about the things that probably seemed mundane and routine. However, it is the mundane and routine characteristics of your household that define your "family dynamics."

Another very important factor to consider about your family is your cultural heritage. How does this affect the way in which you communicate? Does your culture promote more or less emotions and passion? Is it more acceptable to be aggressive, or is it completely frowned upon? Much of this is contingent on your particular household, though your national, ethnic, and racial heritages are all important to take into consideration as well.

Think about it: do you only communicate with people who share the same genetic heritage as you? This is not likely if you live in the United States, which is the world's biggest melting pot. Your interactions likely differ between different groups of people, not solely based on their roles in your life. This may seem presumptuous or racist, but it is not. In fact, it can be a huge positive, as different cultures have different expectations, and communicating even just slightly differently for them could very much be a sign of respect toward them.

Now consider how people in your family communicated with others that they encountered in public; strangers, to be specific. Were they kind and courteous, or snippy and rude? This can be difficult to gauge because, as stated, your inherent bias tells you that the behaviors you observed from the time of being very young are "just normal" and "how the average person acts." When you went to a restaurant, try and recall how your guardian spoke to them, and relate it to how you treat others. While it is entirely possible that someone consciously opted to do the opposite of what they observed as a child, it is more common to naturally grow into those behaviors. This is one of the reasons why an abusive parent is often times found to have been the victim of abuse in their own childhood.

Author's Experience

I was very much blessed with a great family. I had a mother, a father, and an older sister with whom I was only 19-months apart from in age. When I was in fifth grade, my mother's parents moved in with us, and lived there until my grandmother's passing 10 years later, and my grandfather's four years after hers.

To say that we all were close would be an understatement. My mother's family came from Cuba, having fled communism in the 1960s, so my sister and myself were the first generation on her side to be born in the United States. My father's family is White-European, but several generations have lived in the United States. This side of the family is notably less expressive and affectionate than my Cuban side, which is in-line with the culture from each side, as my father's grandparents were blue collar workers who were notably stoic.

In contemplating all of the different factors that I encouraged you to take into consideration from your own family, I can say that I was blessed with a very loving and supportive household. I certainly inherited more behavioral traits from my mother's side of the family, being more quick-triggered and expressive in many different situations. My sister, while very expressive, is much more like my father and his side: more stoic, professional, and less spontaneous.

My family always emphasized working hard and treating others with respect, just as we ourselves would like to be treated. As I grew up, I would hear key phrases that my parents would say to strangers, and I have found myself using them in addition to some words and phrases that I have employed myself while in casual, everyday encounters. After years of reflection on my upbringing and how it has played such a huge role in my life, I have come to the strong belief and conviction that being self-aware of how your family has influenced you directly affects your behavior, especially as it relates to communication.

This conclusion was only further emphasized while I worked as a social worker, encountering children with behavioral disabilities in their households, helping address dysfunctional behaviors and problematic family dynamics amongst all members of the unit. There were times that I had to tell a parent point blank that their behavior was problematic and dysfunctional to the rest of the family. Doing so was obviously quite difficult, and admittedly required quite a bit of courage to muster up, but by then I had built enough trust to where I felt able to do so, as they had accepted me as a member of their family, in a way.

No matter what type of home environment you have been raised in, do your best to think back objectively about your culture, the traits that you did and did not inherit from your guardian(s), and how they continue to influence you and those around you to this very day.

Outside of the scenarios presented earlier, consider how family members in your household communicate with each other on a regular basis; not just growing up but even now if you still interact with them. Consider how much mutual respect is or is not there, and whether or not any reunions or encounters are anticipated or dreaded. Remember: introspection requires that you evaluate your own behavior, not just that of everyone else. Try and think about whether or not you are communicating love or dread, support or degradation, hope or despair. As we will discuss further in this book, communication goes so far beyond what you say.

Chapter 2:
Friends/Acquaintances

Even more diverse than the variable of family is that of friendships. It is this author's hope that everyone reading this has a strong network of friends that go beyond just a good time, and provide you with the kind of support that proper friends ought to. If you feel as if you do not have any close friends, or maybe you struggle to meet new people and only call a few people your casual acquaintances, let us start this portion discussing some ways of communicating an opportunity for friendship.

When entering various social situations, always make sure to look like you are relaxed and approachable. This does not mean that you have to always look absolutely perfect. This idea is in no way a shallow, surface-level piece of advice. Which of the two sounds more approachable: someone clean-cut with a simple and stylish outfit, or someone unkempt with leaves and branches in their bushy beard, sporting a long, dirty, dusty jacket? Who would you rather have walking in your direction? The first one, right? Exactly; I rest my case.

In all seriousness, making yourself presentable on the outside is the window of opportunity for people to get to know who you are on the inside. The term "dress to impress" should not be shrugged off. Having a strong appearance according to your setting is a form of communication in and of itself. You are telling everyone around you that you are able to dress accordingly, that you are confident, and even that you are capable of basic human hygiene. The latter third of that sentence may sound like a joke, but sadly, it is not.

If two people show up to the same job interview, one dressed in a suit and the other dressed in sweats, who do you think is more likely to be seen as competent and professional? Certainly the one in the suit. Even if the applicant in the sweats has every degree under the sun and a world of knowledge to contribute to the workplace, they will not be accepted into the professional environment because they do not see the importance of wearing that experience on their sleeves, at least long enough to get people to listen to them speak about it.

When approaching social opportunities, also consider what the intention of the others in that setting are. For example, what do you think is the main goal of people at an organized speed dating event? This is a bit of a trick question, as there could be a wide spectrum of motivations for going to such an event. One person could be looking for something fun to do on a Saturday night, another might be looking for the be-all end-all one and only love of their life. Still others very simply might be interested in "just saying" they have tried the experience of speed dating, and yet another might be looking for a no commitment type of relationship.

You do not have to be able to enter a room and read every single person's mind. Rather, reading the room and seeing if there are others who share your intention of meeting new people is the best way to go about it. Look at their body language; what are they trying to communicate to others? Are they with a group of their own friends in the corner, or are they sitting alone and appearing lonely? Do they themselves seem approachable? Being able to communicate is important, but the ability to read what others are trying to communicate is an equally valuable skill.

By this point, you may be nervous and not know how to approach new people. Start with the basics of first interactions. What is the main thing that you are expected to do when confronting a new person in American culture? Shake their hand, hug, or simply acknowledge the other person, and then verbally introduce yourself. However, the key to a welcoming introduction is making the other person feel that you are even more interested in getting to know them. If it makes you feel any more confident, ask for their name if they do not give it. Maybe even say it and ask if you pronounced it correctly. Most importantly, let them know that you are happy to get to meet them.

If you are approaching a new potential friend, ask them to discuss something of interest to them. Again, make them feel valued and appreciated. If you are able, relate something they say to your own interest. This does not make the conversation about you or take the attention from them. Instead, you are initiating a back-and-forth dialogue with them. Additionally, you are developing a sense of relatability. If everything goes as planned, you have been able to learn their name, make them feel appreciated, and also make them feel understood and related to. Hopefully by this point in the conversation, you have gained a sense as to whether or not this is someone that you would be interested in getting to know better. If so, then great. Exchange numbers and set up a time to hang out, possibly engaging in a pastime that was discussed in your conversation.

Perhaps you are experiencing the opposite sentiment. Maybe you are not feeling as enthused about getting to know this person. This does not have to be for any reason beyond that you do not feel a sense of chemistry with them. These kinds of things can actually be boiled down to the simple sentiment of "not feeling it." If so, all you have to do is move on. Unless you have set plans to meet with this person in another setting, you have no commitment to them. However, this is not a free pass to be rude about it. Simply let them know that it was nice to meet them, and move on to the next person.

Author's Experience

One of the most compelling parts of being a musician is the natural chemistry that comes as a result of playing with other like-minded musicians. When engaging in a jam session, it is an incredible experience when you are able to collaborate in real time with someone. Being able to improvise a piece of music is a fun activity, but it escalates to a higher level when you jam with someone that you have musical chemistry with and you can work off of one another's abilities and skills to make something incredible. Very much like a romantic relationship, the more you play with another musician, the more you pick up on the traits and quirks that makes them unique. Once you have worked together to get to a more advanced level, you can collaborate and do some really incredible things together even right on the spot with no planning.

However, the unfortunate reality is that this is not a universal phenomenon. Not all musicians have chemistry and work well off of one another. Even if both parties are very talented and skilled, and even if years of practice are put into the musical relationship, none of it matters if there is no natural chemistry.

By the time that I had reached my senior year of high school, I had been playing guitar for a few years, having been mainly self-taught. Up until that point, I had not met many other musicians, and was not skilled enough to really develop a quality collaborative relationship even if I had. That year, twin brothers joined my senior class from having been homeschooled. I grew fairly close with these brothers, as they were musicians as well: one on piano, and the other on guitar.

I was closer friends with the other guitarist than the pianist, and spent more time playing guitar with him than with the pianist. In fact, we played together almost every day during free periods or after school. Our dedication to growing musically was so strong that we would often skip lunch just to have more time to practice. Even after playing so frequently together and working to advance our abilities, and even though we always had a good time, there was still a lack of solid, unwavering chemistry between our guitar playing. Yes, we were able to get through a song well enough; and yes, there were a ton of songs that were go-to jams that we could perform well. However, it was not explosive.

Eventually, we went to different colleges in respectively distant regions of the country. Since then, I've continued to practice and develop my own musical abilities. My friend unfortunately put the guitar down and took up other pastimes. Although we may not have blended musically, we fondly recall the time that we worked together and collaborated as a tremendous learning experience for both of us.

If you are struggling to meet new people, it is this author's hope that the last section was helpful for you. However, for those others who have a network of friends but are looking for better and more effective methods of interpersonal communication, than the rest of this chapter is for you.

Another hope of this author is that you have found your group or groups of friends to be of quality and substance. You may have seen that the title of this chapter highlights both friends and acquaintances, so it is worth defining both before moving forward. An acquaintance is generally referred to as someone that you are socially familiar with, and that you connect with and have a fun time with, but are not particularly close to or do not see very frequently. A friend, however, is someone whose time with you goes beyond simple and occasional social encounters or activities. A true quality friend is someone who is with you through both fun times and difficult ones as well. They are the person that is ready and willing to check in to make sure everything is okay, or helps you get through a particularly difficult breakup.

For most of us, we at least have a few friends, and they mostly land somewhere on the spectrum between a casual acquaintance and a "loyal-to-the-death" best bud. There is nothing wrong with having people in your life that you know are not necessarily there for you in tough times, but you can at least trust and have a good time with. These would be more in line with the term "fair-weather friends," and having such people in your life is not necessarily a bad thing. The only danger with such friends is when you are unable to recognize the role that they play in your life. In this case, there is less of an emphasis on communicating as there is on reading and interpreting what others communicate to you.

When you bring up something that you are going through to a group of your friends, how many of them listen in and engage? How many others tune out and start to look at their phone? If you have found yourself going through a difficult time, have you contacted anyone to ask for advice or maybe just to spend time with them, and they seemed to disengage? Maybe none of these have happened, and you have very simply found yourself not wanting to call them during a tough time. Believe it or not, these are all ways in which you can interpret the nonverbal communication being emitted by those around you. Although it is not unheard of, it is still very rare for someone to bluntly say, "Look, I'm not all that great at (or interested in) helping you. Maybe you should talk to someone else."

To be fair, there may be times where a friend might verbalize that a professional clinician, such as a therapist or a substance abuse professional, would be a better, more helpful outlet. Additionally, someone might be honest and express that they are generally not good at providing advice, but are willing to help in another way. However, someone nonverbally expressing their disinterest in helping you is more common than an explicit verbal expression. Sometimes these actions include when a heaved sigh escapes, an uncomfortable shift in their seat takes place, a yawn and/or a stretch, the aforementioned phone comes out, or maybe the classic eye roll occurs. Try not to get on their case. After all, you do not necessarily know the reason for them disengaging. Just learn from the experience and find other people in your life that provide better support for you.

Tough times aside, let us consider how you and your friends communicate with one another when times are happy which, hopefully, is the more consistent mood and sentiment when interacting with them. It can be easy to fall into the trap of being goofy and reckless with your friends, and all friend groups have their own inside jokes and rapport, without a doubt. However, just because you and your friends have a good time does not warrant disrespect.

What does this mean? Essentially, we can poke fun at each other in a way that is fun and friendly, but we have to be able to read the situation and make sure that we do not cross any boundaries or make them uncomfortable. Lack of formality does not translate to lack of respect. The two are not interchangeable.

Clearly, this is a fine line. What is seen as fun, and what is seen as offensive? Obviously, this is going to change from person-to-person, but there are a few consistent ideas to keep in mind that are universal.

Firstly, what is it that you are poking fun at? Is it a personality flaw? A physical defect or deformity? A mental handicap? Are you making light of a tough life event? Hopefully none of these is the case. Although your friend might make light of these on their own, that does not give you the right to do the same. Additionally, there is often no way to tell how they internalize these items. Perhaps they make fun of it on their own in order to cope with an insecurity, or maybe they are just trying to come off as "strong" in order not to seem weakened by it. Who knows; perhaps this is something that has caused tremendous amounts of trauma for them. It is not your responsibility to address such things unless you are offering to help with it.

The previous examples of sore points are fairly extreme, so what of those outliers that are found somewhere in between mild and brutal? What of the subjects that seem perfectly innocent to laugh about, but turn out to be difficult? How do you avoid these, and what do you do to handle them if they come up?

In trying to avoid such tricky subjects, there is a simple piece of advice that can save you from a lot of trouble: think before you speak. Sure, we have all heard this to the point where you might dismiss it, but there is something to be said for it. When with a group of friends, or maybe just one friend, there should be plenty of moments where you are not speaking. Either the other party or parties are speaking, maybe your server just arrived at the table and stopped the explicit conversation, or maybe there is just a natural moment of silence that is not being obligatorily consumed with needless words to fill the silence. If you have a funny thought, and it has not been a recurring item between you two, just take a very quick moment and run it through a mental filter. Will this hurt their feelings? Have they expressed a struggle with this subject or something similar to it in the past?

If this is a close friend, consider that you are one of the people that knows them best. If you confide in one another, think about the fact that there are probably things you know about them that no one else does. Maybe they have approached you in the past about a frustration in their relationship, or maybe their family did something to upset you. Ideally, if this is indeed a close friend or a "best friend," you are likely to know enough about them to know what will and will not affect them negatively.

Also look at the person's body language. If someone says something about them, such as poking fun at their appearance in a seemingly playful manner, do they laugh the way they always do in other humorous situations? Do they shift in their seat? Do they end up changing their clothes or fixing their hair when no one seems to be paying attention? There are so many intentional or involuntary signs that someone is not particularly comfortable with something, and reading these at all times is essential in being the best communicator possible.

With all of this in mind, how do you deal with a situation where you have overstepped a boundary. As they say, "hindsight is 20-20." If you are not familiar with this phrase, it essentially means that you can better perceive something when looking back on it. Another idea behind this saying is that it is easier to see into the past than the future. Being that most of us are not mind-readers, this much is pretty obvious. However, it is still admittedly difficult to assess how a situation played out, even if it is already in the past. As such, the previous bit of advice about playing out a scenario mentally and ahead of time may not prove to be successful. Just because something that you would like to say survives your own filter does not mean that it would make it through someone else's.

If you find yourself wondering if something you said offended someone, do not be reluctant to simply ask them. Approach them in private if in a group setting, or just ask them when the conversation allows the opportunity if one-on-one. Something as simple as, "Hey, I hope what I said earlier about _____ (use your imagination) wasn't hurtful. If it was, I'm sorry; I didn't mean for it to be." Hopefully, their response is a quick, "Oh, that? Not at all! I thought it was funny," and you both feel better about it. If things do not play out in this way, and their response is something more to the effect of, "Yeah, I wasn't crazy about that" or "Yeah, that wasn't okay," do not panic. Although they may be hurt, do not let your world fall apart as a result. Hear them out, and let them know that it will not happen again. Go ahead and also let them know that you are always more than willing to listen and let them vent if they need to. Everyone makes mistakes, but you can learn so much from those errors.

As stated, all friends have their own special rapport and quirks. Enjoy them, as they are the defining component of what makes friendships fun and special. They are also the cornerstone of any fun time that you have with them. Cherish your friends, respect them, and be there for them in the way that any good friend would be and should be.

Chapter 3: Dating/Relationships

We just finished discussing the importance of friendships, some important components of respect amongst your friends, and how to properly communicate as a good friend ought to. How much more important are all of these variables when considering them within the context of romantic relationships? I'll answer that for you: they are the pillars upon which all the weight of your relationship rests. As a result, it is the breaking point by which your relationship will either stand stable or crumble to the ground. If you do not believe me, just consider how many times you have heard someone, either in your own life or even just in a movie or television show, say that their relationship could not work because of "poor communication?" It is so common that it is practically a stereotype. What it all comes down to is that a successful relationship is based on strong communication and strong trust, so let us discuss some of the components of starting your relationship the correct way.

For the sake of this discussion, it should be established that long-term relationships, such as marriages or longer commitments, will not be discussed. This includes long-term dating relationships as well, as there is hardly enough time to even discuss how to communicate during the first few times going out. Dating relationships are used as the model for this section in order to help and promote good communication from the beginning of a potential relationship. As such, "dating" is operationally defined and conceptualized as mutually organized and agreed-upon interactions with a potential significant other, taking place prior to an official relationship being established. Additionally, no genders or relationship structures will be specified in this chapter in order to assist you as the reader with immersing yourself into the information and scenario. Try to personalize the following chapter. Think back on your past experiences, and consider both what went well and maybe what could have gone better, as well. Read this chapter with a first-person perspective.

Why is dating being discussed? Firstly, dating in and of itself is a form of communication. You and the person you are dating are immersing yourselves into different environments to see if you get along, can work together, have a good chemistry, and other crucial factors. If you find yourself physically, mentally, and emotionally attracted to someone that you are going out with, there is a delicate balance between playing things so cool that you are not interesting, and pouring your heart out about wanting to marry them. Dating can be very difficult, no doubt, especially in the beginning.

From this very beginning, the first impression is absolutely vital in order to establish yourself as respectable and a valuable investment of your date's time. Naturally, you should be cognizant of your appearance in every setting, but especially when approaching the possibility of a date, or a date itself. Just as was discussed at the beginning of Chapter 2 on the subject of friendships, it is not shallow or insincere to note the value of proper appearance, and it is not a subject that will be shied away from throughout the rest of this book. As stated, being approachable and pleasant to look at is the window of opportunity for people to not only get to know you, but for people to WANT to get to know you.

I as the author would be doing you as the reader an injustice if I did not address this point head-on, as your appearance is a form of communication in and of itself. Dressing well and taking care of your personal hygiene is a way of telling the world how competent and well put together you are. There seems to be a belief out there that you should be accepted for who you are, regardless of these factors. People are more than entitled to this belief. However, think about the standards that you want in your own partner. Think of it in simple terms. Let us break this down into some small hypotheticals.

Just a disclaimer before we go in: this message is going out to both men and women. As a result, the scenarios represent that the same standards should be held for both genders, as the subject of respecting your partner is an equal yoke to carry. If you consider yourself gender fluid or of an alternate, non-traditional gender, this message is still meant for you.

Imagine that there has been someone that you have encountered off-and-on over the past few weeks, maybe even months. You have been too shy to say anything in approaching them, and they have yet to approach you. Finally, you muster up the courage to approach this person and strike up what turns out to be a lovely conversation with them. Much to your surprise and excitement, this conversation concluded with the mutual decision to go out on a date, and you settle on the following Friday evening.

You may have played it cool in their presence but proceeding into the elevator led to a devastatingly embarrassing dance and a jump that would have nailed a classic freeze-frame in an '80s sitcom. Of all of the fantasies that you have run through in your head, you never ACTUALLY thought that you could have come this far, and even getting their phone number excites you.

The week and a half leading up to the date might as well have been a year, as it felt like an eternity. There is so much anticipation and so many thoughts of this person being so dreamy and appealing. You even go to bed early every night leading up to it in order to make time move quicker. Every desire is to text the other person and check in, but every instinct says to hold off. When they text you that Friday afternoon to confirm plans to meet at the designated restaurant, your heart jumps out of your chest as every bit of your energy is invested in resisting the temptation to respond right away. Finally, after waiting another painstaking 45 minutes, you respond with a simple confirmation.

When work finally lets out, you make a mad dash back to your place to get ready. You open your closet and pull out the pre-hung outfit that you have had in mind for this special evening, having planned it out in your mind long before the date was even set. This perfect outfit is still on wire hangers and has a plastic covering draped over it, as you had gotten it dry-cleaned days in advance. Once it is laid out on the bed, you cannot help but smile, as it looks even better than you had imagined, and is perfect for the nice but relaxed restaurant atmosphere that you plan on meeting your date at.

Both before and after your shower, you pull out all the tricks. Every component of your "special occasion" facial regiment consumes your bathroom counter as you struggle to suppress your anticipation and nerves just enough to remember if the blackhead mask comes before or after your hydrator. Thankfully, you kept your earbuds in so that you can verbally command your phone to set a timer for the whitening strips that you are applying. If they come off even a few seconds early, you might lose your date's interest forever!

By some miracle, you manage to get everything you wanted to done by 7:30pm, with more than enough time to make the five-minute walk to the restaurant. Before walking out the door, you go into the kitchen and slowly drink a glass of water to help calm your nerves. After pouring the water into a glass and taking a sip, you catch your reflection in a distant mirror, and again cannot help but smile as you observe all of the hard work that you have just put into your appearance for the evening. After all: your date is worth the trouble and anxiety.

Eight o'clock rolls around, and you are left standing at the established street corner rendezvous just near the restaurant. Another look in both directions does nothing to reveal your date, and the worst case scenarios start to pour in from your imagination. Just as the worst thoughts seep in, someone across the street waves and runs over to you. The summer sun had just set, and the streetlights are not enough to reveal this stranger until they are right in front of you. Much to your shock and dismay, this "stranger" is actually your date.

They chose to wear a wrinkled and stained white t-shirt and worn and dirty jeans, and their hair is an absolute mess. The stunning, perfectly formed being that you had been so excited to get to know has vanished forever. This is especially surprising, as they had always looked so nice and well put together when you would run into them.

Despite all of this, you do your best to suppress your initial shock and force a smile and greeting. In returning the greeting and apologizing for being late, as they had lost track of time watching this amazing new show that had just been released on a streaming platform, you get a sample of their breath. It seems as if each word of their absurd spiel starts with a prolonged "H" as the unfortunately familiar stench of greasy pepperoni and cheese fills your nostrils. Your notably poignant sense of smell is only confirmed by what appears to be a fresh stain of red sauce on their now off-white t-shirt.

As you are still trying to gather your thoughts and contemplate all that is unfolding right in front of you, your date goes in for a hug. In most situations, this is not something you would mind at all; only this time, you are met with a waft of body odor from their exposed armpits. The heat and sweat from their shirt does not help matters as you retract and have the awful idea of playing an old trick to escape this nightmare.

Once away, you pretend to fumble for your phone and simulate answering it. As you speak to no one on the other line, you mentally try and think of the wildest scenario just to make it seem authentic. Usually, the idea of lying is so repulsive and is not even considered a viable option. However, this is such a special exception that you do not even question.

After a few forced lines of imaginary dialogue, you "hang up" the call and turn back to your date, letting them know that an awful emergency has come up, and that you have to head out. Your date has a somewhat surprised look on their face for a second, but shrugs and says it is not a problem.

This scenario was comically exaggerated at points, but these kinds of events are all too common. How devastating is it to put all of that work and time into getting ready to meet someone and not having the favor returned for you? This idea goes so far beyond not having the skills or money to dress well.

As stated, the date had always looked nice when encountered in the past. The issue at hand here is more so a matter of a lack of mutual respect, which is the very reason that the date was cut short and did not end up following through.

What sense came to your mind when you reached the point in the scenario where the date arrived? What did you think as the adjectives of their appearance rolled in? Did you get the sense that the date cared about making a strong first impression to the other? Probably not, but not for any shallow reasons that may come to mind. In fact, it was even noted that the restaurant they planned on going to was casual and did not require formal attire. For all that we know, a t-shirt and jeans may have been perfectly acceptable outfit choices.

The issue is not the style, but the substance. This person did not care enough to change into a clean outfit. By their own admission, they were more interested in devoting their time to the new streaming series than in preparing for this date. Even if the alternate outfit involved another t-shirt and another pair of jeans, at least it would have been clean. Additionally, this person could not even be bothered to put on deodorant and brush their teeth, much less straighten their hair, out of respect for the other person.

The date did not end because you were picky and shallow; the date ended because you are good at both communicating and reading communication. As a result, you read into this person's choices and were so very disappointed to find out that they were not very invested in going out with you. However, you are a determined and motivated person that does not let this get you down, and you manage to go on some really great dates with someone with much more care and investment in creating and communicating a strong first impression.

In the coming section, we will discuss other methods of positive and negative nonverbal communication within the context of the dating world.

Author's Experience

All growing up, I had the tendency of sticking with the same friends and friend groups, not having much interest in venturing outside of my comfort zone in that regard. As a result, I continued this bad habit into my college years, even despite a very socially successful four years of high school. The new city and state, as well as the thousands of unfamiliar faces around, made it difficult for me to venture outside of my core friends for the first two years at the school. Since I struggled to meet new people and socialize with others, I did not find many opportunities to meet girls to ask out.

During my first year of college, I met the cousin of one of my new friends, and mustered up the courage to ask her to coffee. She agreed, even despite us not having gotten to know each other too well. We went out and had a decent time together, though there was not an explosive connection between us. Still, I enjoyed my time enough to ask her out again.

The next few dates were progressively more and more disheartening, as she seemed more invested in her phone than in engaging with me. I struggled to pick up on the hints, and would still ask her out, almost out of obligation to myself. As I went to pick her up for one date, she saw a friend of hers from a distance and enthusiastically asked me if she could join

37

us to go out to eat. My heart sank as I said yes and, to no surprise whatsoever, she was completely consumed with speaking with her friend the entire time. In fact, her friend would even stop her and engage in some dialogue with me, almost out of pity.

Needless to say, this was the last time she and I went out. What is funny is that I was not even too disappointed by the experience. In fact, I came out of it learning a lot about nonverbal cues as well as how to hold someone's interest on a date.

When looking back on each time she and I went out, I initially feel stupid for not doing a better job at picking up on the vibes that she was sending out. However, I have to take into account that I had not developed much experience dating and still had a lot to learn. Also, there were many times prior to that last date where she was very engaging and she and I had some strong conversations. She was always polite and courteous, not being rude to my recollection. Additionally, there were many times where she would see me on campus and go out of her way to greet me. These positive moments seemed like enough to warrant continuing to go out, ignoring the signs she was sending that she was not interested in being more than friends.

As stated, I came out of these dates having learned so much about engaging and keeping someone engaged and interested while on the date. We all have embarrassing stories to think back on, and would certainly cringe if given the unappealing opportunity of looking back on some text messages we have sent out in the past. Despite what may feel like shame, there is actually nothing wrong with having these types of exchanges.

Dating is one skill that you can practice and practice and still make plenty of mistakes. The key comes down to being able to communicate properly, both verbally and nonverbally. Do not get down on yourself if you struggle, as even I, as the author of this book on interpersonal communication, am willing to admit my mistakes and have a good laugh about it. Rather, learn from your mistakes in the past and make for a stronger future for yourself and the people you will encounter.

This "Author's Experience" portion highlighted another important piece of communication: body language. Just as we discussed the importance of reading the body language of a friend when you make a joke at their expense, it is undoubtedly even more important to learn how to read the body language of the person or people that you are going out with. Although everyone has their own individual methods of communication, there are a few common universal signs that you can pick up on.

Firstly, the most basic and common one is that of actual verbal interactions. Are the words and topics flowing out in such a natural way that nothing is remotely forced, or is each verbal interaction forced? Sadly, I have to even ask if there is any conversation occurring at all. If not, there is no one to blame. Just as was discussed in the chapter about friendships, some people do not have a natural click and chemistry, and that is okay. You can be very attracted to someone physically but not connect with them on a mental or social level. Certainly, the opposite of this is true. There can be some people that you get along with so well, but there is no physical attraction between you two whatsoever.

If the conversation is engaging and natural, there are a few nonverbal cues to look out for. A commonly cited one is the orientation of the other person's body. Are they pointed toward you, or in a different direction altogether? Some people suggest that you ought to look at their shoes and see if their feet are pointed in your direction, but it is the belief of this author that the entire body is more important, and there are a few reasons why.

Therapists are encouraged to be cognizant of their body language when engaging in a session with a patient or client. One of the worst things that a therapist can do is to use their body to make a patient feel shut out. This might happen if the provider has their legs crossed, if they are leaning too far back, or if their arms are crossed over their chest. Even facial cues are an important component to be self-aware of, as a scowl or a furrowed brow can come across as irritated, impatient, or judgmental of whatever is being discussed.

Within the dating world, there is a certain art to subtle communication. Oddly enough, there are things that your date probably wants to have communicated, but really does not want to hear it said. This may seem contradictory, but it makes sense when you break it down. For example, you may find someone attractive on the first date. However, you probably do not want them to dramatically confess their unwavering love for you right from the start. It would be a gross understatement to say that doing so would be a bit intense to start things out in this way.

To be honest, you may very well feel as if you do indeed love the person you are going out with. In fact, there may be some cases where there is a natural and healthy obsession with your partner leading up to going out with them. You may be so convinced that this is someone that you hope to spend the rest of your life with. Regardless of your emotions, very few people want to hear that from the start. If you feel such things, then consider dating an opportunity to nonverbally communicate with them that you are worthy of their time and affection. As stated at the beginning of this chapter, dating in and of itself is a form of communication between yourself and your potential significant other. Treat them with respect, have a good time, and nonverbally communicate your interest without scaring them away.

You may feel a sense of powerful attraction to this person, but be careful not to confuse love and infatuation. Contrary to what many suggest, infatuation is indeed a form of love. However, it is also a form of fantasy. The way you defeat this euphoria is to date someone and figure out if you two have chemistry, as well as to look beyond your physical attraction. Both fortunately and unfortunately, dating can show some of the less desirable characteristics in someone. You may still be infatuated when you say that you do not care, but you know you love someone when time has not turned you away from someone's quirks. You can especially be in love if their quirks match your own.

How you go about showing nonverbal interest to your date is difficult for this author to say, as this is a subjective matter. In fact, it is one of the very things that either continue or end dating relationships, as different people want it done differently. Some people are open to different approaches, and some are so particular that they struggle to find someone as a result. One thing that I will say is that if you have an opportunity to go on a first date with them, you have likely done something right up until this point.

There are those rare, weird occasions where someone goes out with you despite not being too interested in you to begin with. If you go out on enough dates, this will likely happen at some point. It is okay. Do not let this speak to your own self-worth. Do not let this make you feel as if you are not worth going out with or that no one is interested in you.

On a separate note, it is important not to become too invested in the person you are going out with at the beginning of your time with them. We just discussed cases in which you are indeed invested deeply, and you may be hoping that things work out on a long-term basis. It is fine to wonder this; after all, what is dating if not an experiment? In fact, you should be wondering and thinking about the future with this person. On the other hand, for your own mental and emotional health, it is important not to put "all of your eggs in one basket." This translates to not becoming so excited at the prospect of being with this person that your world falls apart when they decide not to continue with you and go out with someone else instead. You may feel some anger, sadness, resentment, or a plethora of other emotions; however, this is entirely their right, just as it would be your right to respectfully break things off and go with someone else if the roles were reversed. As a result, you must have some level of restraint and self-control when going out with someone.

Back to nonverbal expression; different people are looking for different things. What is appealing to some is repulsive to others. Even characteristics that may seem completely universal, such as being friendly and charming, may be perceived as annoying and uninteresting to some people. In dating someone, it is not your responsibility to figure out how to reach someone else and adjust to their style in order to woo them. Quite the opposite, actually. The very purpose of dating is to figure out whether you two will have chemistry and meld well together. If you do not meld, then it is simply time to move on.

In conclusion, just as dating takes practice and development, so does interpersonal communication. All that you can do is your best, and you should not hold yourself to an impossible standard. Contrary to the popular saying, practice does not make perfect. Practice causes improvement, and you will improve on both your dating and communication skills the more you work on them.

Chapter 4:
Co-workers/Superiors

One of the components that made "dating" a difficult subject to discuss is the idea that dating is so subjective, especially in the day and age we live in. Different people have different standards and expectations for their partner. For instance, a traditional etiquette cliché is for a man to open the door for a woman, or just letting a woman proceed first in general. However, in our current society, some women might be offended by this behavior, finding it demeaning and presumptuous toward their sense of independence. All of these factors make dating very inconsistent from person to person.

Interactions with your co-workers and bosses are very different. Transitioning from such an open-ended discussion to a context with more universal expectations can be jarring, but we often have to make quick appearance and behavioral transitions. If you have a short commute to work, for instance, you go from being in your pajamas, if any clothes at all, straight into whatever consists of your work uniform or professional attire. Vice versa, we are always more than able and willing to transition out of our professional live to relax and have fun.

Before we delve in, it should be noted that this portion will focus mainly on behavioral interactions, as Part II of this book is more focused on communication within environments with less of an emphasis on individuals. As such, this chapter will discuss some appropriate interactions to consider and maybe some to leave behind as well.

When you consider the term "workplace" or "professional environment," it can mean a lot of different things depending on the type of industry and role that you are in. For one, it can be a stereotypical office environment full of fake plants, water coolers, and cubicles as far as the eye can see. On the other hand, you could work in a labor job where most of your day is consumed with heavy lifting and even heavier machinery. Still another person might be in a bustling, chaotic hospital, running from patient to patient, putting out every fire that comes up.

Regardless of your line of work, it is next to impossible to have a job where there are absolutely no interactions with others. Even that famous streamer on the Internet still has to get paid by someone, and if they run into a technical issue, there has to be someone on the other line for them to call and get it fixed. Even that legendary singer has to have a band to back their voice up, a stage crew, sound mixer, manager, producer, record label, and other people to support them. No matter what your career is, you inevitably must interact with somebody at some point.

Although different work environments have different rules and expectations, there are still some universal standards to abide by. Treat everyone equally, do not harass anyone or make anyone feel uncomfortable, no physical aggression, and do not talk smack about your bosses. Is this where it ends, or is there more to being an appropriate worker? Hopefully by now, you answered the latter.

Working with other people requires a team mentality. Even if you prefer independent work, and even if most of your day is indeed consumed by independent responsibilities, you still have to be able to work with others when the need arises to do so. What does this mean? This does not mean that you have to be the leader and do everything yourself. Additionally, it does not mean that you ought to default to letting someone else take the lead every time and try to simply get by through choosing the easiest tasks to do. Essentially, every workplace and every team will require a different dynamic. The very definition of a "team player" should be the ability to adjust to what is needed, not choosing the easiest option or forcing yourself to be the leader.

Good chemistry in a workplace team can be seen when several people are able to come together, and everybody is able to utilize their own individual talent to contribute toward the completion of a project or even multiple ongoing things that arise. Notice how that summary does not designate specific roles to each person, like a school's Student Council would. This person is the "president," that person is the "vice president," and this one is the "secretary." No need. There is enough of that in your company itself. How much better does it sound when you restructure it conceptually to say, "this person takes care of writing contributions," or "this teammate works on any publicity or communication for the team." If someone knows their role and is good at carrying it out within the team, why designate a leader out of pure obligation? Take turns being the leader. If you are in charge of writing, and there is a team project that places a huge emphasis on writing contributions coming up, volunteer to step up to the plate and do so naturally. If someone takes issue with it, offer to discuss it with them and hear their concerns.

Think back on school, when there was a group project or presentation to complete. How many people stepped up to the plate to contribute? Were you ever in the position of being a designated "group leader" and having to assign responsibilities for each member? How well did that work out? How much of that work did you have to do because people did not step up and contribute? Did it even get done?

What are you even getting at with all of this talk about group projects? What does this even have to do with interpersonal communication with co-workers? Yes, we know, communicate with the group and do your part! We get it!

Correct. Communication with the group is an essential part of working in a team. Letting your co-workers and teammates know what you are doing and how it is going is a must. However, what I am getting at goes before any of this. When you first sit down with either a new team or for the first part of a new project in an existing team, try to discuss more than just the project itself. Speak about your abilities and how you can make the vision happen. Aim for so much more than just "getting it done."

Communicating with co-workers about your talents and abilities is not bragging, and does not require modesty. When asked in an interview what you are good at, and where your strengths lie overall, you do not want to shy away from an answer and settle with something like "Oh, nothing really, I guess." Similarly, when working with co-workers and teammates, make sure to communicate what you can do and how you can contribute.

Communicating your abilities, talents, and strong points goes so far beyond the singular context of group projects. In fact, your direct supervisor should know your strong points, even before your job interview. Many people list their strengths onto their CV and/or resume. As stated before, letting people know about your abilities is not pretentious. In fact, you should be your own advocate in the professional realm, letting employers know why you are an asset that stands above the rest. You are a valuable commodity, and you ought to market yourself as such. However, with all of this in mind, it is just as important to be able to communicate your weaker points.

A classic, stereotypical question asked during interviews is one that sends chills down the spines of many applicants: "What are your three biggest weaknesses?" As stated, there is nothing wrong with letting people know either what you are particularly skilled at, or what could use some work. Answering this question does not mean that you have to list things you are blatantly bad at. Rather, you should focus on points that could use some improvement.

Consider this scenario: an interview with you for an exciting new job opportunity has been scheduled. In preparation, you dress to the nines and are confident as ever. You printed off your resume on several sheets of expensive paper, and are ready to disperse them to anyone who is willing to look it over. After waiting for about ten or fifteen minutes, you are called in to the board room with three suits; you straighten your stride and walk in with a smile on your face. Once introductions and formalities are through, you are asked to name your three biggest strengths. The way in which you rattle them off and explain your strong suits appears as a strength in and of itself. Just as you finish up your monologue, internally feeling as if you practically have the job, you are hit with the question about your weaknesses and what you would improve on yourself.

What is running through your mind at this point? What approach should you take in addressing this? How do you communicate the things that need work without undoing the impressed expressions on your interviewers?

It is the conviction of this author that the question of your weaknesses is more important to answer well in an interview than any inquiry about your strengths. This question is like a delicate, expressive, and strategic ballet dance. There are certain beats to hit. Making an error, as well as abandoning formality and structure, could result in an understudy having to take over for you (i.e., not getting the job).

Before getting into how to construct this answer, as it should be tailored to your own individual self, let us first consider what the absolute worst-case scenario is. Other than sitting and saying absolutely nothing, or going running out of the room in hysterics, one of the worst answers you can give is to say that you do not have any weaknesses at all. Not only is this an indisputable lie, as every person has things to improve upon, but it communicates to your interviewer(s) that you lack a sense of introspection. Additionally, denying any need for improvement also denies yourself the ability to improve at all, which is clearly communicated. Another very concerning and negative message that this communicates is that you are self-absorbed, which is easily one of the most undesirable personality traits in the workplace, or really in general. How can you be expected to work alongside others well if you see yourself as perfect and, thus, superior over everyone else?

During an interview, your answers and the ways in which you provide them are picked apart and evaluated, especially as you grow professionally. Being successful in an interview is not contingent on reciting the "perfect" or "textbook" answers. Rather, the best answers are the ones that balance professionalism with personality and expression. You may have filled out an application, you may have had a pre-screening interview with a recruiter, or you may have networked with someone in the company, but this is really the first opportunity to show these people who you are and all that you have to offer, both inside and out. As such, let's try and break down how to develop your own answer to one of the trickier interview questions.

Very simply, first consider what you really could have done better in the past. If you have never thought much about this, you ought to take the time for that introspection, as every good employee has recognized at least some areas of improvement. Even though this seems like the question to just make something up for, it should be one of the sincerest parts of your interview, so take the time to think about this. Reflect on your own performance, any feedback from previous bosses, and what you would like for yourself. After all, you are putting yourself out there to try and snag a new job, so your own professional development must mean something to you.

Next, try to phrase it in a way that is less blunt and more eloquent. It does not need to be a scripted line or a verbal essay by any means. You just want to try and avoid being too blunt and short. "I'm not good at filing things" leaves a lot of ambiguity and further questions. What do you think is the problem with ambiguity and room for interpretation in a meeting?

At this point, you want to try and phrase your answer(s) to reflect a desire for growth and development. Continuing from the example in the previous paragraph, let us look and see about promoting this desire to grow. Additionally, feel free to throw something in there to imply that your hard work shines in other areas. How about this:

"Occasionally, I have a tendency to leave things like filing to the end of the day because I tend to prioritize the more immediate issues first."

Now let us break down each component of this and discuss what worked and what could be better. Starting off with the opening word choices of "Occasionally, I have a tendency to..." This is a nice way to preface the statement. You are communicating that your "weakness" in the workplace is not something that happens frequently, but you are willing to admit that the coming sentence does indeed happen sometimes.

Next "...leave things like filing..." can be problematic because there is still some ambiguity to this. Sure, filing itself is mentioned, though the plural use of "things" makes this phrasing imply that more work was being neglected. Recall what was said earlier about not wanting the imagination(s) of your interviewer(s) to run wild. Keep it specific. Keep it narrowed down.

The following phrase "...to the end of the day..." is good in that it establishes that work is not neglected for another day or week, implying that work is completed daily. However, perhaps a better phrasing such as "later in the day" would be more suitable here.

Finally, the last chunk of the example concludes with "…because I tend to prioritize the more immediate issues first." This is a major saving grace in the statement because it portrays you as responsible for the more important components of your workday. It also tells your listeners that you are competent in being able to determine what is and is not worth your main focus and time.

Now that we have discussed some of the concerns and opportunities for revision, let us try implementing all of these points and rephrase the statement:

"On occasion, I have the tendency to put smaller tasks to the side if I am consumed by bigger, more immediate matters. However, I am always sure to complete them before leaving for the day."

Wow. This may not be dramatically different from the other sentence, but it is composed so much more comprehensively and responsibly. It encompasses a weakness, but rebrands it as a strength. At no point does it sound like a cheap escape or sidetrack from the original question; it acknowledges a weakness, but simultaneously and immediately makes mention of how it is being (and will be) addressed moving forward.

Author's Experience

So much of this chapter has focused on the importance of communicating your strengths and weaknesses to co-workers, superiors, and interviewers. Particular attention has been paid to the questions of strengths and weaknesses respectively, as this is truly your first opportunity to communicate and market yourself as an asset to whatever organization you are fighting to be a part of.

After graduating with my Bachelor's, I went straight into my Master's program. In doing so, I worked tirelessly to find a job. Even applying for Bachelor's-level jobs in my field, no fish were biting at the lines I was casting. After finally connecting to a position in my field, I went back to the Google Docs document that I was using to keep track of all of the applications I was submitting, and found that I had submitted for more than 150 positions in all sorts of different industries. Despite the frustration of not being able to find work, I was blessed with the opportunity to practice my interviewing skills and develop my presence and communication when first meeting a potential employer.

The problem with my experiences is that I eventually had to apply for work outside of my degree. Any retail or labor positions within a ten-mile radius of my home were sure to receive an application. When I would be lucky enough to snag an interview anywhere, I was so disheartened when I would be turned away, as I was overqualified for many of the positions offered to me. There was even one job I interviewed for where all I would do is haul people's "junk" out of their home. Again, I was turned away for being "overly qualified." Something had to give.

In practicing my interview skills, I realized that there was more to my inability to find work than simply being "overqualified" for each position. I found that I was not using enough introspection, and was a little stiff and green when answering questions. As I loosened up my physical mannerisms, I researched and produced a series of typical interview questions, creating and customizing a set of personalized answers to each of them. This only proved successful because they were actual, genuine answers based on previous work experiences.

In referring back to the question about my greatest weakness, the question that has been discussed ad nauseam this chapter, I formed and phrase my truth into a prepared (not scripted) answer:

"Sometimes, I have a tendency to become fixated on the little details and tasks that comprise the big picture, losing focus of the big picture itself. However, I have been working on reeling myself back and getting back to that big picture."

I was proud of this answer, as it really is the truth, even to this day. Most interviewers reacted fairly well to this response, though a few would inquire further: "Okay, how so?" or "Give me an example of that." The first few times I was asked this, I froze up and probably gave a bad response that did not properly encapsulate or represent my answer. However, as I continued to practice and practice, I eventually reached the point where I was able to conceive answers and examples on the spot.

Just as is the case with everything else in life, interviewing is no exception to needing practice and development. How difficult is a task to be able to answer questions in a formal and professional environment, simultaneously having to add your own personality and twist into the content? As I experienced for myself, the key to this balance is to find your stride, then to work on making it look and sound as natural as you can, evidenced by both your body language and the actual content of what you are saying.

Professional Maintenance

Up until this point, we have discussed working in a team, as well as reviewing some opportunities to make a solid first impression during an interview. However, what happens after you are hired? How do you maintain the first impression image that you put on full display, engaging in ongoing communication of your competence?

One way that you can do so is to ask as many questions as needed. When you first start in a new position, there is nothing wrong with asking a lot of questions. In fact, that it in and of itself is a method of communicating to those around you that you are excited to get started, learn, and contribute your responsibilities correctly and honestly. It also tells the people hearing or answering the questions that you are not prideful understanding your place as the new hire. Ignore anyone who suggests not to ask many questions.

If you are retaining the information that is presented to you in response to your questions, the frequency of future questions will inevitably shrink. You will begin to understand the finer details of your role in the organization, and your communication of being willing to learn through asking questions will eventually shift to the communication of competence through the quality of the work you are outputting. However, this progress and growth does not mean you are past the point of asking for clarification or assistance in an area. You should still be willing to ask for assistance with completing a task or project. Just because you have been let loose to be independent does not mean that you should feel uncomfortable with approaching someone and requesting some help.

When starting a new job, it is natural to feel overwhelmed by the new work environment, new people, new location and subsequent commute, new responsibilities, and other tasks thrown your way. However, what many people do not often acknowledge is how you can still become overwhelmed several months after starting, after you have already adjusted and completed all your trainings. Sometimes you might be in shock of how time has flown over the past few months, and it can come as a jolt when it hits you.

Do not worry if this happens. If it does, always be ready and willing to confront your boss or co-workers about it. Work as a team and keep everyone in the loop so that they can assist you in any way needed. Asking for help does not make you weak. In fact, it makes you stronger for being willing to admit that you are not perfect and can use a hand. Someday when you have more time and experience under your belt, you will certainly return the favor by being there for a new hire, supporting them in the same way that you were supported in the past.

Author's Experience

Not long ago, I was hired to work for a new company. This was a hugely exciting opportunity, as I was working extremely hard to both get out of the company I was working for at the time as well as the field I was in overall. What was especially exciting was that the very role I was onboarded for involved utilizing skills and creativity that my previous supervisors would demote and not encourage.

Upon starting the job, my new manager explained the extensive six-month project that I would be taking on. Essentially, I would be updating and building a provider network comprised of therapists for employees to be able to utilize when needed. In doing so, I was given free rein to establish a system of keeping credentialed items up to date, clean out old files and reorganize the drive where it was all stored, recruit various providers around the United States, and other important tasks. Both my boss and my co-worker were still fairly new to the company and department respectively, so they were inheriting a mess of a network but did not know much about it. It was a thrilling opportunity, and I sank my teeth into it right away.

Along the way, one of the challenges that I faced was that every single provider's credentialing information was outdated, and although the department thought they had a couple of hundred providers in their network, I might as well have started from scratch. Based on proper documentation, there were actually zero active providers, so it did not look good when I would present numbers to my boss.

Although the low figures were not my fault, as I had only just joined the company, I was quietly struggling with reaching out to all of these providers. The biggest flaw in my new system was the ways in which I was reaching out to providers to request updated information. I did what I could to send personalized emails to each one, specifying what items were needed, with the thought that giving them a particular set of items would speed up the process. It did not, and I found myself sifting through hundreds of emails and responses, completely overwhelmed.

I did not let my new team know about how much I was struggling with this until a meeting I had with my boss. She asked if I needed help, and I expressed to her that I was confident in my abilities and the system that I had put in place, but was worried that providers were not responding fast enough. Rather than becoming upset or impatient with me, she simply brainstormed an idea for she and my co-worker to help send out some email blasts to all the providers simultaneously.

Feeling internal frustration and disappointment in myself, I sat down with my boss a day or two later, apologizing for things not working out as planned. I will never forget her facial expression when I initiated this conversation. She furrowed her brow, bobbed her head backward, and said "Sorry? Sorry for what?!" The next few minutes were consumed by her reassuring me that everything was fine, and that she and I are still getting to understand one another's styles. She also noted that this was a big undertaking, and that there were some growing pains and a learning curve to work through before the project was able to really flourish.

The project ended up turning out well, as the efficiency of the new system that I was able to create was put into effect immediately. Once my boss and the head of the department fully understood how there were no providers actively credentialed, the growth that occurred was able to be seen as significant. All in all, this experience proved to be a blessing and a hugely important lesson to not be afraid to ask for help.

In conclusion, different work environments have different demands on their workers. Even within those environments, which will be discussed in Part II, different positions that comprise the organization's ladder require completely different things between two employees. Two people might work in the same area and office, but might be expected to have two completely different appearances. No matter where you are in your professional life, you will always continue to learn how to best communicate with those around you in the work environment. Just as was said about interviewing, it takes time and practice. You will find your stride. You will find your voice. You will find your success.

Part 2: Environmental Communication

In considering the topic of communication, particularly interpersonal communication, so much emphasis is placed solely on the interactions with another person. However, an important factor that acts as a driving force and a huge influence in the methods of delivering your communication is that of the environment that you are in while communicating. Yes, the people you are communicating with are the biggest factor, but what you say and how you say it is hugely influenced by where you physically are when the need to communicate arises.

For instance, you may have a close friend that you see many times throughout an average week. As such, you have had the chance to take time with them and develop a strong rapport. You have a similar sense of humor as well as a similar overall outlook on life in general. Many times, one of you knows what the other is thinking even before it needs to be said. Despite being on the same wavelength and knowing how to properly communicate with one another, the things you say and do are going to vary depending on where you are. Regardless of your chemistry with them, you are not likely speaking to them the same way in a church as you would be in a bar.

This coming section is unique in that it takes what we discussed in the first half about communicating with people and groups of people, and turns it around to how communication relates to the environment that you have been immersed in. For this reason, the term "environment" is being operationally defined as your physical surroundings based on factors such as geographic location, locational culture, and surrounding inhabitants.

The specificity of this definition is very important because different places have different standards. Using the example of church, there is a whole plethora of different church cultures based around factors of religion, denomination and/or sect, location, primary racial or ethnic culture, primary age demographic, and local culture. One city can have a whole variety of churches ranging from a small conservative church primarily comprised of an older congregation all the way to a mega church located in a stadium with a primarily younger audience and ear-piercingly loud praise music. For this reason, you cannot make generic statements about "behaving in church" and expect it to be universally applicable.

The same goes for work environments, which were discussed in Part I. When mentioning work and professionalism, many of us default to imagining a generic office with sterile lighting, though this is only a small representation of the vast array of different kinds of work environments out there. For some people, work looks a little different every day, as they may be working from different locations or sites. Some people work primarily or exclusively from home, so it is perfectly acceptable to slip into some sweatpants as a pseudo work uniform.

All of these factors go into the importance of being able to read your environment and tell how your behavior will adjust. With that said, it is worth noting that the ability to quickly adjust your behavior and communication techniques and approaches on a whim is invaluable to being successful. Knowing how to change your affect from casual to formal or even formal to casual is essential in being able to communicate well to a larger variety of people.

Why is this important? What if you work from home and are not particularly social, thus making social interactions less important or frequent for you? Firstly, you still need to be able to reach people. Humans need some exposure to other humans, even if your personality prefers solitude. Even if the extent of your social interactions takes place while playing video games in your bedroom, or maybe chatting online with a faceless person on the other end, we need some kind of companionship.

Additionally, you need to be able to advocate for your own needs. If you get seriously hurt or injured and need to go to the hospital, you need to be able to express to the nurses, doctors, and hospital staff that you are in need of medical attention. When you go to order food or coffee around the corner, our society places a great deal of value in being able to interact with your server and/or cashier in a civil and polite way.

The following is a collection of chapters focusing on how different environments affect your communication and suggests some ways to easily know what to expect when entering that environment. One thing to look out for is advice on how to not let your methods inappropriately cross over from one environment to another. If our loved ones and close friends know us well enough, they might comment on how you are letting another environment bleed into your current interactions.

As we get ready to jump in, start to think about your own core list of environments. During the average week, where are the main places that you go? Who do you associate with? Are there any groups outside of family, friends, and co-workers that you interact with regularly? How do you transport between these different environments, if at all, and how much time do you have to transition out of that place mentally? Start to process these questions and personalize your own perspective as we start off with looking at the most personal and intimate of places: the home environment.

Chapter 5: Home Life

As you begin to think about the interpersonal communication within your home life, first reflect on your structure. Are you married? Any children here or on the way? Are you still living with your own parents? Any siblings? Who raised you? What racial, ethnic, and/or social cultures does your family hail from? Is your family religious? Did your parents split up or divorce? What role did your grandparents play in your life, if at all?

These are actually very few questions of the infinite that comprise the complexity of family culture. As discussed in Part I's portion on interacting with family, no two families are the same in their methods of interaction and family dynamics. What makes the following chapter different is that these dynamics take place within the environment of the home. This is notable because when you are at home with your family, and there is not company over, very little filtering or barriers are present. No social formality keeps you from expressing what is on your mind, as all of the social constructs from everywhere other than home remain locked out. Depending on the values in place, or maybe even the lack thereof, a family dynamic may either promote complete transparency or formality under the roof. Wherever your family falls on that spectrum, the home is the ultimate citadel of these values, and they are carried out in their rawest forms in between your four walls. How can you be considerate of your loved ones in this rawest of forms?

What can you do to communicate toward others in a way that is thoughtful and loving, while still natural and relaxed?

This can actually go back to the home itself, and the way it is oriented. You have the ability and the right, as do the rest of those present in the home, to find a designated spot to serve as a go-to area when you are feeling on edge or even just need time to yourself. As the old proverb says, if you have nothing nice to say, don't say anything at all. This could not be more applicable to home life interactions. Few things are more unsettling than when there is unending tension in the home and those present feel as if they cannot escape it. After all, where can you go and unwind if not home?

What does this designated space look like? There is no possible way to suggest something that will be universally applicable, as different living spaces and quantities of people within the home vary wildly. As such, it cannot be said concretely that you ought to designate a bedroom, as you may reside in a studio apartment. Even a bathroom cannot be designated, as one's space may only have one bathroom for everyone to share. However, a bedroom serves as an excellent place to unwind if available to yourself, as your body is wired to unwind there every night when you go to sleep. Frankly, this space can simply be the corner of any room with a chair if needed. The only criteria for it is that you feel a sense of sanctuary there turning everything and everyone off to relax and destress as well as being able to seclude yourself from others as much as possible. For this reason, a room with a locking door is preferable but, as stated, this is not always an available option.

Once you have this designated space for yourself, it is important to communicate with your family calmly and respectfully about it. Inform them of your space's location in the home as well as the intended purpose of it. Let them know how you plan on making the most of this space and how you will go about using it. This advice is delivered to you as the reader in vague, general statements, as how this information is communicated is contingent on family dynamics that cannot be generalized. However, what can be said universally is that it needs to be delivered with the same level of respect that is expected within the moments that you need to utilize this space.

It is extremely important to note that this space is not meant to be used all of the time. If one is going through a difficult time, especially if you are young and angsty, there is the possibility that you might fall into the habit and routine of going straight for this space to replace interactions with others on a daily basis. Doing so would defeat the purpose, as this is only a suggestion to regulate your emotions and promote healthy interactions with others in the home.

So much of what we need from the people we live with can take work within ourselves to self-regulate. However, in doing so, we have to know ourselves well and find out what does and does not work for ourselves and our own mental health.

Author's Experience

Having worked as a care coordinator with children for many years, I had to subsequently work with many different kinds of families. A care coordinator is essentially a behavioral social worker, and I would go into the home of a child client and helping both the child(ren) and their families function normally. This was notably tricky because many of the families, if not most of the families, had mental and behavioral disadvantages of their own. When this is the case, there is a lot of enabling of behaviors, as the parents may not have the cognitive ability to know any better. Past environmental factors have a big role to play as well, as the parents of these parents may have instilled problematic behaviors.

With all of these factors in mind, one of my main roles as a care coordinator was to work with both a child and their family, observing dynamics and working together to try and suggest resolving these. Most of my work would be done with the child directly, and many times I found myself encouraging seclusion in order for them to be able to handle their anger and sadness. A goal as simple as the child voluntarily going into seclusion seemed, and often was, too unachievable and unrealistic. The problem was often that the child would have to remove themselves to cope because of the parent triggering them. Clearly, if your parent is enabling negative behaviors and triggering you, you are prone to not being able to control your emotions. Our society is constantly reiterating the importance of listening to your parents and obeying what they ask of you, but what do you do if your parent is the direct cause of your emotional struggles?

One case that was particularly intense involved an older teenager who was adopted into a large family. He was the youngest, and all of the other children with special needs had moved out and started their own lives, so his mother was exhausted. As she struggled with physical ailments of her own, tension grew in the house, as my client was particularly aggressive. The cognitive issues that he had been born with made proper communication and expression difficult for him.

Additionally, no one could tell whether he struggled to comprehend and retain information from the world around him or if he was a chronic liar, as he had a frequent tendency to make up absurd stories or completely reword what someone had said to him.

As time went on and efforts proved fruitless, the only goal that I was able to truly work on with the family was for both the teenager and his mother respectively to inform one another when they were becoming flustered and needed some space. Sadly, this did not prove to be the most difficult activity to get down. There was a point where both parties were able to do this consistently. The issues arose when the other had to respect the wishes of the person who needed space. Tensions had a tendency to boil to the point of physical altercations between them, so having them try and perform this seemingly simple task had the potential to be a matter of life and death.

Despite this family having a large team of supporters to back them, they continued on this circular pattern. I wish I could tell you that I was able to work with them and make things work, though my working relationship with the family ended when I witnessed what appeared to be self-inflicted cut marks on the teenager's arms, and I had to file a formal report. This infuriated the mother, who ended my time with the family shortly thereafter.

The unfortunate truth about families is that some members do not have personalities that mesh well together. Seeing families out and about in the community reveals absolutely nothing about their home lives. No matter how great and perfect a family might look, perhaps to the point of wishing your own family was more like someone else's, you have no way of knowing whether or not the members that comprise said family are able to communicate with one another properly and effectively in a safe and healthy manner. What I came to learn with the families that I was successful with was that people need to be able to work on their own character and temperament as well as finding what works for them regarding self-regulation, long before the time comes to work together as a family unit.

Once you have established your own sanctuary to help you self-regulate, and once you find your own ability to keep control of your own emotions, the next step is to begin working with your family on proper means of communication. As has been stated over and over, only your family is privy to your own authentic family dynamics. As such, it is not this author's responsibility to tell you as the reader how to approach your family or how exactly to go about communicating with them. However, it should be noted that it is absolutely this author's recommendation TO communicate with them.

Next time you and your family are gathered together, let them know of your needs. You have taken the time to discover what does and does not work for yourself, and now is the time to let them know of how you plan on self-regulating. In working on yourself, hopefully you have had the opportunity to consider ways in which you interact with others, and how some help could be utilized. Perhaps it would be helpful if you had the opportunity to be alone in silence for an hour each day, or maybe you need someone to talk to when things get particularly difficult at your job or school. Communicate your findings. Let those in your household know what you have learned about yourself, and how you are growing emotionally.

This suggestion might conjure images in your head of a dramatic sit down around the table. Do not think of this idea as anything more formal than just starting a conversation with your family. Maybe the television is on, but everyone is on their respective phones or tablets. Maybe you all are at the dinner table, and there is not much discussion going on. You can just preface the conversation by telling them that you have been working on yourself and finding what does and does not work for you regarding self-control and mood regulation.

Bringing this up is not self-absorbed or selfish of you, nor does it imply that your family is bad or struggles with communication. Rather, think of it merely as an opportunity to make your home environment more of a pleasant place to live for everyone. Additionally, there is no more close-knit group structure than a family, and it is crucial that everyone do what they can to be honest with each other and let them know about what is going on in their lives. Letting your family know of your needs is merely being an honest member.

Let us consider a scenario. For the sake of making this as relatable to your own experiences as possible, think back on your family structure growing up. If you did not grow up with a family, consider the environment that you were raised in and the people that were present in it. Think back on being a young teenager, only having just started to discover yourself and the world around you. In working on finding what works best for yourself, you have found that secluding yourself in your room right after getting home from school helps you regulate before interacting with other members of the household. You enjoy your family, but you have always struggled to turn off whatever events took place at school earlier in the day.

Despite not being inappropriate about it, as you always let your mom know that you are heading upstairs, she has often called you back down and instructed you to tell her about your day. Despite still trying to remain polite and let her know that you need "a minute" to yourself, she still insists that it is blatantly rude to just go straight to your room after getting home.

One evening, after yet another annoying instance of your mother not letting you have space to yourself, you strike up a conversation at a dinner table. This begins with you asking the group how they like to unwind. Your brother says that he likes to play video games before going to sleep. Your father says that he enjoys watching old television shows after work. Your mother says that she enjoys reading a novel with jazz playing in the background. Finally, your turn comes up, and you say that what works best for you is to be able to lie on your bed and close your bedroom door for a few minutes as soon as you get home. You then turn to your mother and ask her if there is any way she could understand and respect this desire. Much to your surprise, your mother looks shocked and acknowledges that she misunderstood what you were doing, and would do better in letting you have the space you need. Still surprised at this answer, you thank her and acknowledge your own desire to be able to speak with her and spend time with her later in the day, just after you have had the opportunity to unwind.

Thinking about this scenario, you may wonder why the protagonist did not speak with her mother about this in the moment as she was being denied access to alone time. Additionally, why did she speak with the entire family and not just her mother alone?

Firstly, it can be difficult to articulate yourself calmly and poignantly when you are flustered and stressed. The protagonist is probably not anxious to be alone in the room because things went well at school today. When being alone in solitude is the only thing that you look forward to all day, it is easy to become frustrated when you are denied this small request. Taking the time to sit down and discuss this when emotions and frustrations are not high is surely going to ensure a higher chance of success and longevity with whatever is needed.

Secondly, the whole family is being "dragged into this" because communication within the entire family is hugely important. Every member should know about the other, especially considering that people of all ages are constantly changing, sometimes on a daily basis. Although you are particularly requesting that your mother make accommodations for this to happen, you are communicating your own needs to the entire clan for future growth as a group.

Notice how in the scenario, the protagonist initiated a conversation with the whole family on what helps them relax and unwind. Although there was an agenda to open up the opportunity to discuss their own needs, it was still thoughtful to ask each member of the family what works for them and where their needs lie. This also turned out to be a good opportunity to learn about each other, as these might not have been discussed in the past amongst the group.

All in all, these are just some ideas on how to make the home environment more pleasant to be in as well as how to promote growth and development for the family.

What if you are not married or not living with family in the home environment? What if your living situation involves living with other people your age in an apartment or a house? Do the same rules apply for housemates and/or roommates? Well, yes and no. There is certainly a level of mutual respect that is universally applicable to everyone that you live with. Making sure to communicate with one another and work as a team is certainly going to ensure better success and longevity than working against each other. With that said, some would prefer a living situation where each member opts to live independently, only sharing the living space. This is fine too. However, living independently of one another does not excuse the group from still working together as a team.

In such situations where each member of the house is "doing their own thing" so to speak, what ties them together is their mutual place of residence. However, within that environment, there are still expectations in being sure to maintain that space and keep it up. Cleaning up after yourself, keeping the bathroom clean, and clearing out your laundry from the machines when you are done are some examples of this. Having a nice place to live is not one person's responsibility. Everyone has to be able to contribute to keeping everything in order. Even if this just means simply keeping things as you originally found them, it is still important to do your part. In doing so, you are communicating to those you live with that their well-being is a priority, and that you consciously care about contributing to the growth of the home overall.

These may not seem like important values at first, but wait and see how frustrating it becomes when your housemates never clean the kitchen or wash their own dishes, leaving you to do it for them in order to keep this area of the house clean. How frustrating is it when you share a bathroom with someone, and they act as if they have never seen a shower brush before, or even a garbage bag to take out? All of these seemingly little issues add up quickly, culminating to a place of frustration and constant tension.

As has been stated throughout this journey, everyone's experiences and situations are unique and different. No two people live the same exact lives, despite how it may sometimes seem. As such, work on yourself and then work together with your family or housemates in order to promote peace and harmony within the home environment.

Chapter 6: Work Environment

In Part I, we discussed some of the ways in which to communicate with co-workers, bosses, interviewers, and teammates. However, one item that was not discussed was that of your place in your own work environment. Examples and scenarios of the term "professionalism" will play out differently for everyone. As stated, no two people live the same exact lives. With this idea in mind, the term "professionalism" can be operationally conceptualized as being able to adapt and appropriately fit into whatever behavior and appearance your job and work environment demand of you.

This definition may seem rather lengthy and specific, but consider that although you may work in an office, your position may be that of a custodian. If this is the case, you are not going to want to wear a formal suit. You will very much need to wear clothes that can handle getting messy. Similarly, you might also work in that same office as the CEO of the company. Although you have probably dealt with many messy issues over the years, you must dress to the nines, as you are the face of the company. Neither of these examples suggest that one is better than the other. Rather, if we are looking at the operational concept of professionalism, it simply indicates that dressing correctly for the kind of work that you will be completing results in communication to those around you that you are ready to complete that work, as well as understanding what and how to do so.

As we all likely know, there is so much more to professionalism than dressing appropriately. Another easy way to communicate to those around you that you are more than capable of completing your work is to take good care of your designated workspace. Making sure to keep everything organized and in its right place is one of the easiest ways to show your co-workers and superiors that you are not overwhelmed by the work at hand. The moment that you have papers flying around your cubicle or office, or your toolbox is so scattered that you do not know where anything is proves to those around you that you struggle with balance. Taking the time to make sure everything stays organized will not only communicate competence to those around you, but will also help you remain regulated when immersed in the work environment. Take advantage of the tools around you. If you have a smartphone or a scanner, transfer all of those important physical papers to digital form through scanning. If it is not needed, or if you have to think hard on the original intent of something, send it straight to the shredder.

In doing so, keep in mind that there is not a universal method of doing so. In other words, not everyone approaches organization the same way. In fact, doing so takes time and practice in order to find what methods work best for you and the way your mind operates. Hopefully, you have managed to find at least a few ways to keep things at work or at home organized, even just the way you fold laundry and put it into their respective, designated drawers. Even if you are not traditional in your organization and utilize a sort of "method to the madness" chaotic way of keeping things, try to remember the importance of respecting the environment that you work in and maintaining professional integrity.

Just as was discussed in Part I, the content of what you communicate to your co-workers is extremely essential to being able to work as a team. Letting your co-workers know what you can contribute, as well as your limitations and the tasks outside of your wheelhouse, have the potential to determine whether or not your office functions to its fullest potential. However, what consumes the rest of your interactions when business is not being discussed? Are there any personable and fun dialogues taking place? Do you joke with your co-workers and/or boss?

Most of these questions are probably contingent on factors such as the mood that the higher-ups have sought to establish for their staff, the effort that supervisors make (or have not made) to keep things light and relaxed, and even the very nature of the work being done. Many bosses make an effort to get to know their staff on a personal level, and they welcome or even encourage the use of respectful humor in communication between employees.

If you are a supervisor, keep in mind that keeping small talk light and positive communicates to your staff that you are a human being and not a work-centric robot that is only interested in the product of the work being outputted by your employees. Additionally, both taking an interest in their personal lives and respecting their personal needs will likely motivate your workers to go the extra mile when the time comes to do so. Doing so does not disrespect the sanctity of the work environment, nor should there be a looming sense of intimidation for doing so, just so long as the employees can reel things in and take their work seriously when "play time" is over.

For the employees, hopefully your boss emulates the values listed above. It is this author's hope that you work for someone that seems to genuinely care about you and your well-being. After all, doing so increases the chance of an employee's longevity without burnout, as well as their desire to even work for the company. If this is the case, you are not obligated to share more information than you are comfortable with sharing to your supervisor or to anyone within your organization, for that matter. No matter how transparent your co-workers and supervisor may seem with their respective personal lives, there are always things that people refuse to share, and that is how it is supposed to be. Regardless of any statements from people such as "here, we are a family" or "what happens here stays here" there are always limitations to what is and is not appropriate within the workplace.

Clearly, there is no universal code for professional dialogue, as some people are willing to share a little too much information, while others are completely reserved toward sharing any personable dialogue about life outside of work. If you struggle to determine what you should or should not discuss with others within your own work environment, try to observe the different subjects that are commonly brought up by your colleagues and superiors. Observing and picking up on trends is the best form of exposure to find out what works and what does not. Furthermore, you should also see how your supervisor(s) react to different subjects. Look at their body language. Do they smile and laugh along? Do they wince in disgust? Do they furrow their brow in distaste? Do they force a smile while looking as if they are resisting the urge to terminate someone on the spot? Do not feel weird about glancing over to gauge their mood. Whether you notice or not, everyone else around you is likely doing the same.

Along with everything that has been discussed, there is an important component to the behavior associated with professionalism. Mastering the art of self-awareness is essential to not only surviving in any job, but furthermore to thriving. Essentially, the idea behind self-awareness is exactly what the term suggests: an awareness of yourself. However, self-awareness is actually very little about yourself. The entire reason that practicing self-awareness is considered a virtue and skill is because it requires that an individual takes the perspectives of others and considers what they would think of your behaviors, actions, decisions, appearance, and other key factors. Frankly, your own opinions and perspectives on how you are coming across need to go out the window.

Self-awareness is one of the keys to professional success; but more particularly, it is the key to respecting the workplace environment. It's being able to know how to behave and how to make sure that you appear as competent and responsible as possible. This is one of the reasons that professionalism emphasizes the importance of proper behavior. Being able to show some sense of structure and self-control tells everyone around you that you are able to take things in stride, especially when things become difficult. It shows that you are able to hold it together when everyone else around you is falling apart.

There is also something to be said for the people that can "read the room" and be able to tell what is not appropriate. As discussed before, any environment requires people to be able to know what is and is not appropriate, though this is particularly and especially important within the work environment. If you misread the situation and say something very inappropriate, you can potentially be out of work and lose your income. Despite any initial negative thoughts or distaste toward this concept, just understand that this does not infringe on your right to be expressive and speak freely. Every employer wants to be able to hire people with self-control and who are able to practice self-awareness. It is never a good look to problematically stand out.

If you were still wondering why self-awareness is so important, or perhaps having any thoughts of annoyance toward this whole subject, let us consider a scenario where we demonstrate the contrast between someone with a proper sense of self control and another who lacks any sense of self-awareness.

Before we begin this scenario, we will first establish the scene, as this chapter is about the workplace environment. For the sake of this example, our workplace will be a stereotypical office. This office is on the fourth floor of a standalone building in an average town. Visually, there is not much about this environment that stands out. Fluorescent white lighting illuminates the sea of cubicles, which match in their dark shade of flat grey. A fake plant here and there tries and fails to bring life to the space. Essentially, this is the kind of office you see in every movie.

Most of the people here seem as if they have worked at their jobs for a long time, as shown by their collective lack of expressiveness. Most are dressed professionally, or at least appear as if they are trying to. By the dry ways in which people interact with one another, it seems as if most people ride the line between thriving and surviving, just getting by in an average way.

With all of these factors and images in mind, also keep in mind that the people here are very difficult to read. Although there is consistency in drabness, things are bland enough to where nothing and no one is expressive enough to send any signals either way. Start to think about how you would approach communication if you found yourself filling a job in such a place.

Enter two young new recruits. Both of these young, starry-eyed hires are fresh out of their undergraduate programs and are ready to conquer everything that the world has to throw at them. However, despite their professional and educational backgrounds being similar, they come from two very different social situations. The first, we will call Chad.

Our fun-loving buddy Chad was originally from Los Angeles, and grew up under the alluring and leisurely California sun. Most of his high school and college years were spent partying with friends and living life in the fast lane. Despite all of this craziness, he performed well in school, as he was gifted with high intelligence. Unfortunately, never having to work hard in school led to Chad developing a poor work ethic. Since this is his first job since finishing school, he is about to learn this for himself.

On the other hand, Hope is just the opposite. Although she has always been intelligent as well, she never found herself taking shortcuts in school. While all of her fellow sorority sisters were partying with the likes of her Chad counterpart, she had a sea of papers sprawled on her bed and a pair of noise cancelling headphones to drown out the subwoofer of the beat-heavy music downstairs. Rare was any opportunity to go to bed early, as Hope was always dedicated to getting ahead and going the extra mile, taking advantage of any offers from her teachers to look over her work and provide feedback if done early. Additionally, she worked several jobs throughout college, even completing two internships for her degree, so her excitement and enthusiasm in joining this organization was not out of ignorance, as she was also confident in her own abilities, ethics, and efficiency.

Sure enough, as the two of them moved into their respective cubicles and learned the trade, and they both picked up on their responsibilities and daily tasks fairly quickly. The first few months went notably well for both Hope and Chad. The very nature of the work was well processed in each of their brains, and each of their minds were both put to good use as things got started and progressively picked up. After each found their footing, however, true colors began to be revealed.

Very much reflective of her time in college, Hope proved to be an extremely invaluable asset to the company. In addition to her hard work proving her intelligence and drive, her youthfulness brought about new ways of approaching certain tasks. For instance, records had recently been transferred to CD-ROM through a painstaking process of scanning and converting documents. Hope showed the office how to transfer these documents over to the company's shared file drive in a matter of minutes, which brought the office to the current year and increased the entire workplace's efficiency.

Furthermore, everyone that encountered her was greeted with a smile and a polite verbal acknowledgement. Before anyone had a chance to see it happen, she had everyone's identity memorized and greeted everyone by name. There was never a day when she looked unprofessional or underdressed, always appearing well put together and never disheveled. With all of these factors in mind, she found herself thriving in the environment.

Chad, on the other hand, was a different story. As stated, his mind was put to good use, performing the work just fine. Whenever he turned something in, the work was done correctly and his intellect was evident. However, one of the biggest issues that Chad had was his lack of a strong work ethic. Unlike Hope, who was always gung-ho toward getting things done both quickly and well, Chad struggled to get anything submitted on time. He had a bad habit of getting distracted from his work and getting lost on an endless trail of YouTube videos. One of the only skills that Chad mastered while working was the ability to quickly close out his browser whenever someone would step into his cubicle.

With all of these distractions, very little was submitted on time. He would often make up an excuse to his boss as to why it was not his fault. This was particularly frustrating for his co-workers and teammates, who depended on him to do his part. His boss tried her best to be understanding and to give him a break, thinking that he was just a little green after coming straight out of college. Nevertheless, even she could not deny that this version of Chad and the one during his initial interview seemed like two completely different people. All sense of confidence and enthusiasm seemed to melt away when he would burst into her office and frantically explain why the data for the report could not be gathered. "I know you said to have it done by today" he would say out-of-breath "...and I'm sooooo sorry, but the stupid system is moving so slow."

Part of the other major concern with Chad was his lack of mutual respect. Sure, his lack of effort was a sign of disrespect in and of itself; but on top of all of this, Chad was known as the "crazy" guy. He would insert himself into random conversations around the office and make an inappropriate joke. During meetings, he would scroll through his phone and snicker under his breath. What only made this worse was that he put minimal effort into making these actions subtle. Additionally, his attire often seemed thrown together at last minute. Despite having nice apparel and some expensive clothing, it was not often that his tie would be on straight or his buttoned shirts aligned correctly. There were even several instances where he would wear a white dress shirt with a graphic tee underneath and, under the office's fluorescent lights, it was obvious enough that it might as well have been the only shirt he had put on.

One day, the VP of the department came to present some annual figures. Both Hope and Chad were present during this meeting, but assumed appropriately different roles in the meeting. Hope had the opportunity to contribute to the presentation, having taken the data and converted it into aesthetically pleasing and professional graphs. Even despite a certain unnamed co-worker running far behind with the numbers, she still managed to submit this presentation on time as a result of opting to work two extra hours after everyone else had gone home for the evening. The VP even thanked her in the middle of the meeting for putting this together and sending it to him. Hope had always been modest and blushed when acknowledged for her hard work, though inside she was celebrating harder than any of her sorority sisters ever did.

Chad, on the other hand, had come three minutes late to the meeting. While not particularly smooth, this usually was not the end of the world, as people tended to wander in late. As this was normal for Chad, it did not really elicit more than an eye roll. However, today's presenter warranted everyone to come early. Chad's tardiness caught the VP off guard as it interrupted him mid-sentence. As Chad scanned the board room for an open seat, the VP stopped his speech and said "Go ahead and find a seat, young man." His voice did not sound thrilled, but he moved forward as Chad assumed one of the spare chairs on the side of the room.

The night prior, having completely forgotten about this big meeting, Chad had gotten a call from one of his fraternity brothers, seeing if he was interested in going to a party. Naturally, Chad was the life of the party, so he went. Despite his initial plan to limit himself to three beers, one thing led to another and he found himself doing a keg stand. All of his stress from the "work world" melted away with every gulp, up until he found himself trying to stay awake. As if the embarrassment of being called out by the VP had not been enough, Chad let out an enormous involuntary yawn that might as well have shaken the room, as it drew about the same amount of attention. While not called out again for this, the VP shot a look out of the corner of his eye in Chad's direction. This hardly phased Chad, as he was scrolling on his phone, which was perched on his lap.

If there are three strikes in the game of baseball, then this VP must have been a pitcher at one point in his life. This had been enough for him. Though he was not prone to be temperamental or impatient with his employees, nor did he have a reputation as such, he stopped the meeting.

"I'm sorry, ladies and gentlemen. Young man in the back there, your behavior has been completely unacceptable, and I think it'd be best if you stepped out."

To add insult to injury, Chad had dozed off and did not hear this otherwise humiliating call-out. The young woman sitting next to Chad tapped him on his shoulder, and he woke back up and pretended to be paying attention. Needless to say, he was lost when no one was speaking and everyone was staring blankly at him. He turned to the VP at the front of the room, and got a chill down his spine when the looming figure simply said "Out."

Two notable meetings took place following this session. Firstly, Chad was asked to sit down with his immediate supervisor. Behind a closed door, Chad had to explain his behavior today and had to try to conjure up ways in which this would never happen again. The VP of the department was not able to attend this sit down, as he was in the second meeting with Hope. He wanted to meet with her and her immediate supervisor to praise her for adding a certain level of class and poise to this office. Although her time in this position had been short and they wanted her to continue her excellent work where she was, she was assured that continuing her efforts would lead to a bright future.

Fast-forward one year. The office, as described, was a very standard and flat-affected workspace. Nothing stood out, and nothing or no one stood out. However, because of the positive influence that the higher-ups saw in Hope, there was a push from administration to encourage workers to greet one another and to uplift each other with more of a positive spirit. Everyone was on board, and measured rates of depression lowered as people began to demonstrate more respect not only for each other, but for the workplace overall.

The end of the story is not as positive for Chad. Not long after the negative impression that he had left on the VP, IT caught wind that Chad was watching YouTube videos in the middle of the workday. Within minutes of him pulling up a compilation of people getting injured on their skateboards, his supervisor was sent an IT notification. By the next morning when the rest of the department came in to start the day, Chad's once overly decorated and crowded cubicle had been emptied out.

This was an extensive scenario, and took some comedic liberties in order to have some fun. However, the sad fact of the matter is that this is not an unrealistic scenario. If you can believe it, Chad is hardly an exaggerated figure. While the events of the story are certainly comedic in contrast to that of Hope, there are any number of people who struggle to transition from college life to that of full-time work in their respective fields.

The inability to dress professionally, the struggle to also appear well put together and not disheveled, an inability to focus without getting sidetracked on YouTube, making inappropriate and unwanted jokes to co-workers, chronically running late for projects…. With these characteristics listed out instead of put into a story, do they not sound familiar to you? At least one person from your current or past jobs has to fit one of these struggles.

If so, how did they come across to you and your other co-workers? Did they have a reputation that followed them? Any inside jokes or nicknames behind their back? While gossiping about people is wrong, it is unavoidable in most offices. This is only natural; just as a strong and positive reputation follows someone around, so does a negative reputation.

Where do all of Chad's poor decisions fall within the context and ongoing conversation about interpersonal communication? Frankly, it does so much to demonstrate the negative power of behavior over verbal exchanges. With exception to the mention of making inappropriate jokes in the workplace, Chad's poor behavior was behavioral. No mention was made of him speaking out of line, being temperamental, or speaking poorly about others. Consider the impression that he made in the VP's presentation: there were no verbal interruptions made, and he did not take a call (as so many people do during important meetings).

If there were no issues with the content of what Chad was saying, where does the problem lie? Come to think of it, maybe Chad did not have an issue with communication at all, right?

Perhaps Chad knew how to speak to people, but he communicated so much more with his actions than he could have ever done with his words. Chad's downfall and eventual demise was a result of communicating a lack of respect for the workplace. His lack of attention to important matters, his complete lack of interest in arriving to meetings on time or even paying attention once there, his lack of competency in dressing appropriately; all of these things culminate into telling everyone around him "I do not care about my work, nor do I have enough respect for you to achieve the bare minimum."

With this idea in mind, Hope's success seems to make a little more sense. The way she treated people was not only valued within the context of human courtesy, but furthermore, it promoted a sense of development and evolution in the way that the rest of the office operated. Hope took the approach that this book suggested earlier and learned about the way the office operates in terms of how co-workers interact with one another. However, she added to it and went the extra mile to add her own values in there. Her efforts to learn people's names and greet them as such was a value that was not suggested to her by the organization, nor was it a disingenuous effort to merely kiss up to her supervisor.

Before we wrap up this discussion, let us take a look at a small detail that was very briefly touched upon in the scenario. "A certain unnamed co-worker" and their tardiness with getting some needed data for the VP's presentation did not slow Hope's roll, as she went the extra mile yet again to get this data processed into a presentation for the VP. Knowing its value and importance, and not falling back on cheap excuses and blaming other people, she worked two extra hours after work—while having to do so theoretically should have been frustrating and annoying to her, especially when her "unnamed co-worker" was truly at fault for this, she stayed late and thrived. After all, every single person in the office knew that he was too consumed with his Internet videos to do his job. Regardless of the poor decisions of those around her, she refused to let herself get dragged down with them. Also, she did not care that she was salary and would not see immediate financial compensation as a result of her extra work. In her mind, she understood both the importance of getting this done and the significance of doing well for the VP. Good impressions are priceless and cannot be purchased, so she wanted to cash in on this opportunity.

Hope had the drive that Chad did not. Her motivation led her to communicate to everyone she came in contact with that she cared about her job very much. Furthermore, her care extended from her own immediate responsibilities out to the rest of the department. The hard work that she put into both her work and her image absolutely screamed respect for the work environment, which went out as a resounding cry that changed the operations of the office in the long run.

Take a page from Hope's story. Be the change that you want to see in your work environment. Go the extra mile, regardless of the lack of instant gratification for doing so. Maybe you even work for an office that does not commend you for all that you do. That is okay; many of us have worked at such a place at one time or another. Do all of these things anyway. Do your best to bring an air of positivity and teamwork. Hope was not greeted by name, or even greeted at all, for that matter. This did not discourage her, as she did this on her own accord and, as a result, redesigned the standards of the workplace.

Do the same as Hope. Do not let the moods or decisions of others change who you are and who you want to be. In the work environment, or anywhere else for that matter, communicate the best parts of your character and see the amazing potential that can unfold as a result.

Author's Perspective

I have mentioned several times that I used to work in the field of Social Work. For anyone that is familiar with the nature of what a social worker does, it is commonly known that it can be a grueling job. After all, the very nature of what a social worker does involves entering into dysfunctional lives and attempting to intervene by bringing some stability to a complete lack of stability. As such, many (if not most) of the homes being entered are messy and cluttered, which serves as a proper model for how messy and cluttered some of the lives of the clients are. In any event, every social worker must be prepared and professional, even in the most-tense situations.

During my time working in the field, there was a young man who joined our organization. Without disclosing too much information about him, it was immediately evident to everyone at the office that he lacked any and all sense of self-awareness. He spoke his mind about whatever came to his head, more often than not inappropriately, and carried a misplaced sense of self-entitlement. My friend, who was responsible for training him, informed management within a week that he was not appropriate for the job and should not be allowed to continue. However, management in our organization was very poor and never paid any mind to feedback from employees.

The crux of contention came when my friend and this new trainee were in a home, and he could not handle the behavior of a 2 year-old girl, the daughter of the client. After the appointment with the client ended, he demanded that my friend take him back to the office so that he could speak with HR about this. My friend had no idea what he was taking issue with, and we are still not clear to this day. In any event, he notified HR, and management finally woke up to the concerns that my friend had pointed out far in advance. He was gently dismissed from continuing training, and to no one's surprise, he was extremely inappropriate behaviorally when asked to leave.

Not only is it important to practice self-awareness within the work environment, but equally important to know yourself well enough to determine whether or not a certain field is right for you. It was clear to everyone that this man was, and probably even still is, in the wrong field. There is nothing wrong with reaching this conclusion, as it is only a gateway towards finding where your greatest strengths lie.

Chapter 7: Home Environment

In Part I, we discussed some of the components of family life. One of the key points from that chapter was that each and every family has their own set of ethics, standards, and dynamics. No two families are exactly the same in that sense, and it is important to respect the differences of others in this way by keeping an open mind when encountering other groups.

How does this translate to respect of the home environment? Essentially, just as each family has their own dynamics, every household has their own unique set of rules and regulations. Some standards are safe to assume as universally applicable, such as "no wearing shoes in bed" or "turn your light off when you go to sleep." Even still, there are plenty of people who have absolutely no problem with you keeping your shoes on in their house, and others like to keep the lights on in other parts of the house at night for security purposes. When entering a new home, it is always best practice to ask your host when in doubt about something in particular.

However, this does not answer how to respect your own home. We have our own cultures, traditions, and influences inherited from our parent(s) or guardian(s). As such, we set our own rules and standards for our respective places of residence. With that said, there are still some universally applicable, basic standards for respecting the home environment.

Before we delve into these, there are a few things to keep in mind. Firstly, and most importantly, these are a series of suggestions. The terms "rules," "standards," and "suggestions" are conceptually and operationally interchangeable for the purpose of this section. Secondly, these are not black and white by any means. In fact, they are to serve as a basic template for you to build upon and personalize in your own unique way. Thirdly, these standards are not meant to take away from your ability, and right, to express your style and personality through your own living space; just the opposite, actually. These are meant to encourage you to not only set up your space according to your style, but also to keep and maintain it in a consistent and healthy way. It is great if you are able to afford the things you want in a home; but if you are not able to keep it in good condition, what good was all that time and money that you invested into it?

With some disclaimers out of the way now, let's get into these suggestions for respecting your own home environment:

- *Create a vision, and see it out*
- *Keep it clean*
- *Keep it organized*
- *Do not crowd the space*
- *Set rules for maintenance*
- *Take care of what you have*

Let us break down each of these suggested standards into subsections in order to fully explore what each of them entails.

Create a vision, and see it out. As was acknowledged getting into these standards, people want to be able to have the

94

ability to express their personality through their living space. At the very least, you want visitors to find it to be a pleasant place, and to be at least somewhat impressed with your ability to furnish and decorate. This is a form of communication in and of itself. Having style communicates your personality to anyone who encounters your living space. Even just having a barren living space with no décor might communicate to visitors that you are a minimalist who deliberately does not own much.

There is absolutely nothing wrong with this; rather, it is actually quite healthy to take pride in your living space. As such, having some fun with making the most of your space is a valuable opportunity. Taking some time to research different styles and creative opportunities can not only give you some great ideas, but also get you excited and motivated to see it out. Utilize the Internet to be able to see what other like-minded people have done with their own space. If money is tight, look into budget ideas, as there is a world of this online, as well.

One of the key components to this standard is that of consistency. "See it out" does not just refer to the action of making your vision happen. It also refers to being consistent with maintaining a style. Having a mix of modern and traditional furnishings might communicate to visitors that you are not consistent, so it is important to take the time to do your research into looks that you like.

Keep it clean. Okay, you finally have your space completed and you finally feel like your home is coming together. When you come home from work and sit down to rest from the long commute, you look around and feel as if you are in your safety zone. The space almost feels like an extension of yourself, and it brings you a tremendous amount of comfort.

How disappointing is it that it becomes cluttered and messy six weeks after you finished working on it? The hustle and bustle of life got past you, and keeping everything as spotless as when you first obtained it is something that can happen to any of us. In trying to relax each night after work, you may have unintentionally left some items laying around. Again, this can happen to anyone. However, the best way to both respect your space and have it constantly ready for others to respect as well is to keep it clean.

Different people have their own ways and methods of cleaning, so there is no concrete way of establishing how to go about doing this. Additionally, different definitions of what it means to be clean can be found, depending on who or whom you ask. Just try and think of the homes that you see on television or movies. What makes them look so clean and beautiful? The lack of stains, natural light coming in to clean the air, no dirt, lack of items scattered everywhere is what does it. While some lifestyles and perspectives find order and peace within a messy home, most would agree that a clean house is more pleasant.

Furthermore, with exception to the occasional big home project or just having children in the home, keeping a home space clean should not be too daunting a task. If you clean up behind yourself and make sure not to leave things out and about, cleaning becomes less of a chore and more of a maintenance task.

Keep it organized. On the subject of keeping things clean, organization is an equally important component that is often overshadowed. The terms "clean" and "organized" are so commonly lumped together, when in fact, they are two different entities altogether. Keeping clean is a matter of actual cleanliness: preventing dirt, scuffs, marks, wear and tear, stains, and other things you would have to maintain. It also includes how sanitary something is or is not. Organization, on the other hand, is more focused on the placement of actual inanimate objects within a given space.

Take, for instance, a child's playroom. In many homes, such a place is constantly coated in toys and games, proving to be as difficult as walking through a minefield without stepping on a painful obtrusion. While this may be the case, perhaps a guardian is diligent about sanitizing everything in the room and preventing any dirt to be tracked in. This is a clean room that is not organized. Similarly, picture a bathroom where every toiletry item is in its own designated space, but everything that should not be on the floor is gathered. Using your imagination, see this as a case of organization without cleanliness. With these cases in mind, let us define organization as assigning each item in a designated space to a particular area or storage, while remaining easily accessible as needed.

Organization is one area that many people seem to struggle with quite a bit; whether that struggle be finding methods of organization that work with them and their minds or just simply never having to be organized in the past and not seeing the value in it. One struggle that many people cite as to why they cannot either achieve or maintain a sense of organization is because they do not have enough storage space in their home. While this may certainly be the case, it is not a legitimate barrier.

Why is this not a valid reason to struggle with staying organized? After all, by the very definition provided above, you cannot be organized if you do not have a place to put your stuff. Fair enough, but the question then changes: do you have too much stuff? If you think about it, having too little storage for all of your various belongings implies that there is too little home for what you have. There is an easy solution to this: get rid of what you do not need or no longer use. Chances are, you have some old items that have run their course. You probably have some clothes that you have not worn in years.

While the idea of getting rid of some of your items may be emotionally difficult and stressful, remember the phrase that "one man's trash is another man's treasure." With some of these items that you rarely or never use, they may be just what someone else is looking for. As such, think about clearing out some old items as giving back to others. In turn, you will receive storage room and more opportunities to eventually obtain newer, better items.

Do not crowd the space. Going along with the discussion of organization, the recurring theme is "too much stuff." This is certainly the case for many people's homes whose living rooms turn out looking like a generic sports bar franchise. Walls are covered in miscellaneous knick-knacks and old items with no clear theme. Looking back, suddenly the importance of picking a theme with your vision does not seem so irrelevant, does it?

Along with this and the notable importance of keeping things organized, it is worth adding that no one wants to walk through a house and trip over things on the floor. Clutter consuming someone's personal space communicates a number of things to others, and none of them are particularly flattering.

If you find yourself struggling to see the value in decluttering your space, thinking that the perspectives of others should not be valued so strongly, consider the idea that some people in your life MUST know that you are able to stay on top of things. For instance, what if your boss decided to show up for dinner after work? How do you think they would appreciate having to walk through a maze of various items? What would that communicate to them? Would it let them know that you are a responsible and dependable worker? Would they count on you to be able to keep track of all of the various documents and forms that your work requires?

Also imagine that you are engaged to the person of your dreams, and you invited your future in-laws over. Would they see your clutter as a unique form of expression, or would they be concerned that their precious child was about to move into this chaos? What would their faces look like as they have to try and avoid stepping on various knick-knacks and miscellaneous Wal-Mart purchases from over the years? Would it provide them with the reassurance that you can provide love and care to a family, even though you cannot communicate a sense of respect for yourself and your home environment?

Clearly, there is an importance in keeping things decluttered. While it may not be the most fun of tasks to clean, organize, and declutter, you want to communicate to others that you respect the home, you respect their comfort, and you respect yourself.

Set rules for maintenance. Much of the last suggestion discussed visitors coming over and into your living space. The driving point highlighted the importance of setting your space up so that they would respect what you have been able to both achieve and maintain. This suggestion turns the tables and presents you with the task of setting up rules to maintain order in the home so that both you and anyone else that comes into the space can keep it in the condition that aligns with the vision that you have established.

Firstly, set some common and easy to remember ground rules. Things like "take your shoes off in the entryway" or "put back whatever you were using before getting something new out" are good places to start. If you keep a clean floor, the last thing you want is for someone to track dirt in with their shoes. In addition to looking bad, it is not sanitary. Additionally, having the latter rule about putting back things when you are done with them is important in order to keep things organized, while the first is more about cleanliness. See how neither of these rules leave anything up for interpretation? They are clear, to the point, and universally applicable for both guests and yourself.

This last statement is an important point to keep in mind. While this is your space, you must uphold your own rules. No matter how tired you are, no matter how badly you have to rush in and use the restroom, always be militant toward yourself in holding yourself accountable toward the rules that you expect others to uphold. You owe this not only to yourself, but to the respect that you owe to your home environment.

Take care of what you have. Most of us growing up were probably told to "take good care" of something given to us, especially if it were fragile and/or of great monetary or sentimental value. Having a child start taking care of what they are given from a young age is very important, as it instills a value of caution and care. Letting a child wreak havoc and break things, even just for fun or curiosity, is a tremendously dangerous habit to allow. In all reality, it is the start of teaching them the value of hard work and the power of a dollar, showing them that having nice things is earned only after putting blood, sweat, and tears into your work.

With these principles in mind, try to apply them to your own life. Think back on the vision that you conjured for how you want your home life to look. If you have applied this vision to your home and pulled it off, you likely feel a sense of pride and satisfaction in what you were able to achieve. Let us emphasize the phrase "pride in what you were able to achieve." If this is the case, how would your pride be affected if your television fell down and shattered? Would you shrug it off and say "No worries, I don't mind spending another $800 to replace it"?

The pride that you ought to take in your home goes so far beyond simple finances. Becoming frustrated in something breaking is more about the time and hard work that went to waste. Additionally, if your home was laid out to emulate a vision in your mind, think of how incomplete that vision now is without this component present. It is like a puzzle that you complete, despite having lost one piece. Even though that is just a flat black or white piece that looks like 348 other pieces in this gargantuan puzzle, it becomes impossible to look at that puzzle as complete. No matter how elaborate or enormous that puzzle is, your eyes will always jet straight toward that jigsaw silhouette missing.

Take care of what you have earned as well as what you have been given. Even if you receive something as a gift, do not think of it as disposable solely because it did not cost you any money. Just because it was technically free, you should not feel a sense of justification over purchasing another one to replace it.

It is my hope that these suggestions have gotten you thinking about either creating or re-writing claims that you should not care about what other people think of you. I as the author must interject that this matter goes further than you realize. There are times when you should absolutely care about the perspectives of others. In the same way that you ought to keep a clean workspace, as discussed in the last chapter, you must communicate to those around you that you are capable of keeping organized and staying on top of menial tasks in life.

Remember this: cleanliness communicates competence. If you take anything away from this book, this phrase is it. While you may want to express yourself by keeping things scattered around the house, try to remember the points reviewed that people's perspective of you is important within certain contexts. Yes, there is no denying that people can be judgmental and presumptuous. Many come across as vain and only seem to care about material things. However, as you will see in the coming "Author's Experience" portion, there is a level of grave importance to keeping a clean house when having visitors over.

Author's Experience

There are times in life where we may encounter someone whose behavior and choices seem unusual, though it may not be evident whether this person deals with cognitive struggles or is simply "artistic" and quirky. As such, there is a term for someone who is very expressive and tends to step out of typical social norms in order to display their personality: "eccentric." To put this into perspective, think of musicians in the vein of Elton John or Lady Gaga. Both of these artists are undoubtedly brilliant musicians who are strategic in wearing absurd and flamboyant outfits while on stage or appearing at public events. While such people may be going through struggles in their personal lives, their expression is considered eccentric, as their choices are not as a result of poor mental health function.

Within the mental health field, there is a set of criteria to help determine the differences between mental health struggles and eccentricity. These are known as the "Four D's" of abnormality, and include "Distress," "Danger," "Deviance," and "Dysfunction." In the case listed above, the relevant component is that of "Deviance." The idea behind this term is that a behavior "deviates" from the norm. If something deviates from what the average person does, the question then becomes whether or not that behavior is "abnormal." If so, what is the motivation of the behavior?

Lady Gaga wearing a suit made of meat is indeed abnormal and certainly deviates from statistically and socially "normal" behavior. However, the context of her doing it turned out to be a public statement against the "don't ask, don't tell" policy of the U.S. military. Eccentric, yes, but not problematic.

How does this relate to interpersonal communication, particularly in the home environment? One of the most applicable uses of these four D's of abnormality is within the home. When a mental health clinician speaks with someone in an office or other clinical setting, they are only able to assume that the patient's words and reports are correct. However, when a clinician sees a client in the home environment, they have a legal and moral responsibility to report any concerns that can be seen. With all of this in mind, there are things that clinicians are trained to look for in the home.

When entering a home, regardless of whether it is the first time or the fortieth time, a clinician has to observe whether or not the house is clean. Part of the clinical documentation for many organizations includes a blurb that requires a description of the condition that the house was in. Another component that must be considered by a clinician is that of safety. If any water is leaking through the roof or there are sparks coming out of power outlets, it must be documented. If the floor was not clean and vacuumed after something made of glass shattered, it must be reported. If children are present in the home, and there is a severe mess with obstructions such as the ones listed, there is a legal obligation to break HIPAA privacy laws and report this to Child Protective Services (CPS). If CPS is not alerted, job termination and license removal is pretty much an inevitability.

These situations dance the line between eccentricity and mental health disabilities. Some people consider themselves "too lazy" to keep a clean home, some believe they thrive in a messy setting, while others have a predisposition toward struggling to maintain cleanliness. All three situations, regardless of which one is the case, require some level of assistance in order to achieve at least some level of order within the home.

As this chapter discussed, there are times in which one's perspectives and conclusions are very important. This "Author's Experience" portion was less comical and light-hearted than the others in this book only to highlight the extreme detriment of respecting your own home environment. While free expression is good for some things, keeping a mess around your home is not conducive to anyone, especially and most importantly yourself.

In conclusion, this chapter has discussed the importance of respecting your home space from so many different angles and perspectives: potential in-laws, hypothetical supervisors, and friends and family. Who amongst these do you think is the most important person to impress? As was stated, you are the most important person to impress. Yes, giving others positive impressions regarding your cleanliness and subsequent competence is essential to succeeding at whatever you do. However, what happens after the party, when everyone has gone home and you are by yourself? How at peace are you if your friends cancel on you last minute, and you decide to just relax at home? Can you really find sanctuary in an area that is chaotic and unclean?

Show your home the respect that it deserves, and show yourself that same respect as a result.

Chapter 8: Public Speaking

Public speaking may seem like an odd next choice on reviewing different areas. However, something that seems so specific and so rare a need for the average person to master is actually incredibly important. Most people will encounter the need to speak in front of a group of people at some point in their lives, whether it is a small group of twenty people or an arena of 20,000. Public speaking does not only refer to standing in front of a podium and a microphone.

If you find yourself needing to speak in front of a group, chances are that you have something of importance to communicate. Two of the three subtitles of this book come to mind for public speaking: "how to communicate effectively" and "relate to others." As a speaker (again keeping in mind that you are not necessarily speaking to thousands of people with a pre-written script), your job is to communicate your point and/or points effectively. While not necessarily required, a good speaker seeks to relate to his or her audience. You want to win your audience over, so what better way than to speak and present your information in the most relatable way possible?

Where do we start with doing either of these? Well, looking at the basic concept of communicating effectively, say what needs to be said! Of course, it is more complicated than this, but firmly establishing your key points is essential in preventing your speech from becoming too scattered, and you will subsequently lose people's attention. Know what you want to say, then worry about how you are going to say it.

Next, consider the term "speaking." When addressing a group of people, you are "speaking" to them. You are not giving a speech. Public speaking is just that: speaking. When you converse with a friend, you use your own voice. When you speak with your supervisor, you are hopefully more professional than with a friend, but you are still using your own unique voice to speak. This is no different than speaking to a group.

Consider the various Presidents of the U.S. in your lifetime. Despite all of them giving speeches in formal settings and in various contexts, each of them has their own methods of communication. Regardless of the fact that they are reading a pre-written speech off of a teleprompter, they are still communicating in their own individual voices; so much so, that each presidential administration is met with a slew of comedic spoofs and impressions. Although a political agenda and purpose is present, and although their words do not often come from their own minds, everything is presented with a sense of determination and a unique voice. Some have spoken with tremendous confidence and poise, some have utilized a more personable approach as if speaking to families watching on television, while others tended to deviate from their scripts and improvise.

Regardless of what style fits you and your personality best, style is something that needs to be played with and personalized. Reflect on some conversational approaches you have taken while talking with your friend or telling a story. Anything about the way in which you say it stand out? Are you flatter and drier, or are you more explosive and aggressive in your approach? Another thing to consider: do you hold people's attention, or do they go right back to looking at their phones within three minutes?

With that last point in mind, an important question to ask yourself is whether or not there is value in what you are saying. Whether you are about to speak with a group of your friends at a restaurant or present on four years' worth of original research that you have conducted, think about the importance of what you have to say in addition to the aforementioned points of how you are going to approach it. Depending on the context of your content, as well as the intended audience, you may also need to ask yourself if people are even going to listen or care. What is your intention in saying any of this in the first place? Do you hope to help people or maybe inform them? Are you trying to entertain with comedic insights and observations?

These questions are not to come across as harsh. Rather, they are intended to help guide and motivate you. If what you have to say survives the gauntlet and is able to be deemed as valuable and important, you will ideally come out the other side with a stronger sense of determination to communicate to your audience and convey the information that needs to be communicated. After all, remember that this book discusses interpersonal communication, emphasizing the desirable yet admittedly difficult task of working to build stronger relationships. If you are speaking to a group for the first time, set the standards for yourself high and give them a solid first impression. This is especially important if you are trying to professionally network, as speaking is an excellent way of getting some attention drawn to yourself as a valuable and marketable asset.

Author's Experience

Not long ago, I grabbed dinner with one of my closest friends and his fiancée. They had prefaced this dinner by telling me that they had an important question for me, but did not give me any sort of hint as to what it could be. My mind raced leading up to the planned dinner, though I figured that it had something to do with their upcoming wedding. Between my friend's fiancée having to get through the extensive legal immigration process to move to the United States and the COVID-19 pandemic, their wedding had been delayed several times and, eventually, reduced in size as well. I knew I was in the wedding party, and that they would not have a best man, so that was not likely. I also considered that they might ask me to be the godfather of their children someday, but that made no sense since they did not yet have any children, and none were on the way anytime soon.

When the big evening finally came, we all took our time to order and talk for a bit, as they had also just met my girlfriend at the time and were getting to know her. Finally, the big moment came, and they ended up asking me to officiate their wedding. Needless to say, I was in absolute shock, and had no idea what to say. They then explained that I did not need to become licensed, as they were already legally married for immigration purposes.

After accepting this more than generous offer, I did not hesitate in composing the best wedding speech that I could. One problem: I knew next to nothing about officiating a wedding. Although I had been to any number of weddings, as well as having been in wedding parties, I had never assumed any speaking roles. I started off by outlining a few important thoughts, as well as consulting my friend to fact-check some information that I was trying to recall gathered from my countless hours of conversing with him.

Once I had a basic idea of what to say, I began to research some examples of wedding speeches that gave me a good idea of the average length and duration, helping me gauge a good length that would keep everyone engaged and not drive them insane. What I found in writing this was that the most important thing I had to do was keep everything about them and make nothing about myself. Although I was going to be the only one speaking, my job was to redirect the spotlight to them.

The big day finally came around, and I was surprised to find myself more excited than nervous. This turned out to be a good sign, as I had edited and practiced it so many times that I felt what I had to say was caring, accurate, and valuable to the event. Spirits were high for everyone present, and the wedding was absolutely beautiful.

After it was over, I was happy with my cadence and volume, as the wedding took place in a small chapel and there was no PA system for a microphone. However, I found myself so dependent on reading from my tablet that I did not look up from the podium too often. This was further validation to myself that I am more of a writer than a speaker. Even during the speech, I looked at each of them and said the name of the opposite partner when making eye contact with them. One of the biggest mistakes that I made was not including the "I do" portion after wedding vows. I was not sure if these would be applicable since they were already married; and after considering whether or not to put them in, I forgot to ask my friend if he wanted them.

After the wedding, I went to the newlyweds and apologized for not including this portion. Also to my surprise, they both dismissed it, citing the fact that they were already legally married and did not see it as an issue. They said that their vows were the most important thing, and they were both able to give their vows to one another. This came as a relief, as neither of them have a tendency to hide their true feelings about anything, especially around close friends.

Not only was this an absolute pleasure and honor to have done, but also an incredible learning experience. Despite having spoken in public numerous times in the past, most instances felt obligatory and involved subjects that I did not care about. Additionally, this was a new type of presentation that I was not familiar with. I had never even been to a wedding officiated by a friend, as everyone that I could recall going to was conducted by a pastor or priest. This new experience proved to be exciting, passionate, and rewarding.

If you have the opportunity to officiate a wedding, do not think twice. It is a great experience, and I would not trade it for anything in the world.

When considering opportunities for public speaking, do not hesitate to research examples on how to go about doing this. Whether it be a written template online, a YouTube video of a particular type of speech going well, or just thinking back on past speeches that you have seen and heard in person, do not be afraid of being unoriginal just for looking up examples. So long as you do not plagiarize and rob the content of your speech from someone or somewhere else, feel free to see and hear how others have done it. There is nothing wrong with emulating those who have done it well in the past, as inspiration helps you find your own voice. See what characteristics and quirks cause people to consider it great, as well as looking for the effectiveness of what they are trying to communicate to their audience.

The big day has finally arrived. You have done everything in your power to prepare for this opportunity to speak. Extensive research, rehearsals, and rewrites have boosted your confidence, and you feel more ready than you ever will. You gather your things, stride over to the podium, move the microphone to a comfortable position, then absolutely fly through the words that you have written. Before you know it, the six minutes that you had planned are over in three and a half, and you have no idea what has happened. Unfortunately, your audience feels that sentiment, as they are very confused and have no idea what the point of any of that was. All of those great words that you composed and arranged went to waste.

What do you think happened in this mini-scenario? Why did the time fly so quickly? If everything was written down, how is it even possible that you did not take the expected six minutes to complete this? One word: cadence.

What exactly is cadence? The operational definition for the sake of this chapter and the context of public speaking is the culmination of vocal elements that encompass the cadence and style of one's speaking patterns. In other words, very simply, it is how you speak. Notice that this definition does not incorporate the content of what is being said. Rather, it is solely the way in which words are put out for others to hear.

This probably sounds vaguely familiar to you if you read the introduction to the book, where we operationally defined "communication" and, more specifically "interpersonal communication." Although the definitions embraced for all three of these terms are similar, "cadence" stands out from the other two as a result of the factoring of "style" as a key variable.

In the scenario above, the content of what was being said was solid. Not only was it well written, arranged, ordered, timed, and outlined, but it was especially well practiced. There was no doubt that this speaker was prepared with what they had written for their audience. However, what should have been practiced just as much was their cadence. Clearly, with the way things turned out, this was missing from the prep work.

You may be wondering to yourself how someone is even expected to be able to practice their cadence. After all, this is something that is often left up to the audience. Is there an objective way of critiquing yourself and being able to tell whether or not you are on point? Actually, yes there is, and it is not too complicated.

One of the first things you ought to take into account when composing your speech is determining how long you will be speaking, or how long you ought to be speaking. If you were not given a template or informed as to how long your portion is, simply do some research as to how much time is spent on the average speech of whatever you are preparing. This can be tricky, especially if you do not have much experience speaking and have very little ability to gauge your own cadence.

If this is the case, there are a couple of things you can try doing. Firstly, reflect back on any instances where you may have been speaking extensively. This could have been engaging in a telephone conversation, giving a presentation in school, or even just talking with friends and telling a long story. In hindsight, do you recall whether or not you shot through what you were saying quickly, or did you drag your words out? Has anyone in your life ever done an impression of the way you speak, or even just simply made a comment about it? If not, it may be just as easy to call up a close friend or family member.

Going along with this, you may be left trying to figure out how you should go about your writing. Should you err more on the side of keeping it short in order to allow you to add to it if need be, or should you go the complete opposite direction and add everything you can possibly think of, then trim it down as needed?

This is a difficult question to answer objectively, as it is a subjective matter. If you have outlined the core of what you plan on communicating and feel as if the aforementioned "gauntlet" of testing your key points' significance was survived, then consider writing excessively. Consider, however, that writing in a greater amount can result in some trouble deciding what is and is not more important. In this same way, writing too little can also be tricky. If you have all of your important key points laid out, it may prove to be tough to add fluff and extend it if what you have already written seems to be effective and communicative as is. However, as stated, your decision is contingent on what you know about yourself and your own writing abilities.

Also consider recording yourself speaking. Grab a book off of the shelf, dust it off, and record yourself reading a page or two of it. If you do not have a designated audio recorder, a basic feature of almost every piece of technology is the ability to record audio. Feel free to first read through the passage that you are about to recite in order to familiarize yourself with it, then go for it!

When you record yourself for the first time, try your best to resist the temptation to look at the timer, or even the time itself. The key to recording yourself initially is to get the most authentic take in order to judge how to move forward. Once the recording is done, try to endure the inevitable cringe we all go through when we are not used to hearing our own voices, and think about how it flows. Is it pleasant to listen to? Are there pauses at each comma and period, or does everything sound like an incoherent run-on sentence?

Punctuation is not only an important tool for spacing out thoughts and statements in writing, but is equally as important when speaking. Punctuation serves as a visual cue to let yourself have a second to breathe, and to give your audience a chance to comprehend what is happening. A very quick and easy way to lose your audience's engagement is to overwhelm them. If someone is rambling onstage without having even a moment to take a breath, many might lose interest and pull their phones out. Even worse, they may dismiss the speaker as seeming like they do not know what they are talking about, and simply overcompensating in order to sound important and knowledgeable.

One of the most important things to remember with cadence and a commonly cited tip when speaking in public is that you always want to err on the side of speaking slower. Just like what happened in the scenario, the speech tends to fly by, especially if you have it well versed in your mind and are very familiar with the content and flow. There is nothing wrong with taking a moment to breathe at certain points. Consider putting a little mark in your notes at certain intervals to remind you to breathe or take a brief pause break.

The more you expose yourself to other speeches, the more you tend to pick up on the comfort and confidence radiating from experienced speakers. It is amazing how some people have mastered the balance of speed, a middle ground between fast and slow; comfortable, if you will. Intertwined into their speaking flow are brief moments where they might stop and look around. Most notably, many speakers do this at the beginning of their speech, just before they begin speaking. Having just walked up to the podium or microphone, they might get their notes adjusted, then take a moment and scan their audience. Many would consider this a power move, essentially communicating that they are not intimidated by the sea of faces before them. However, it is also a valuable opportunity for the speaker to take a moment, gather their thoughts, and not rush into what has been prepared to say.

With all of this advice, what about those who struggle with stage fright? How does someone who deals with anxiety, even at the mere thought of being in front of people, get through and exhibit confidence when they are shaking in their boots internally? What is there to even be afraid of? Many people would say that they are afraid of looking stupid in front of a large amount of people. Nothing irrational about that. No one wants to be remembered as the person who vomited on stage when trying to give a speech.

Some people are actually afraid of much simpler, easy mistakes, such as stammering. Unless a mistake is very evident and problematic, a quick stammer is easily forgotten in most situations. Truthfully, if you force yourself to be absolutely perfect and not try to keep things natural, you are more likely to mess yourself up. Additionally, you will look stiff and unnatural, which is easily much worse than stammering.

So let us discuss some techniques to reduce overall nerves when getting ready to speak. Firstly, the ongoing and recurring theme of practicing excessively has been discussed ad nauseam. One of the most common fears is that of the unknown. This is one of the reasons that people are afraid of the dark, as there is no light to reveal what may be right next to you. Do not leave yourself in the dark when it comes to preparing to speak. Review the material. Practice reciting it both aloud and mentally. Record yourself, and even listen back to it. Do anything you can to get to a place where you are almost tired of what you have prepared.

What about nerves toward being upfront in the presence of your peers? How do you cope with any number of people looking at you and listening? If what we have discussed up until this point has not been enough to make you feel prepared, start to consider some common techniques that people cite. One significant one is to not make eye contact with anyone in the crowd. You may want to try and make sense of your surroundings and your audience by scanning the room as discussed before, but try to avoid direct eye contact with members of your audience.

It is probably safe to assume that each reader has engaged in deep eye contact with at least one stranger before. If you walk down the street and lock eyes with a passerby without any interaction or exchange, it can be very odd and unsettling. However, how much more uncomfortable is it when there is pressure on you to perform and deliver? Naturally, this can become very intimidating, so try not locking eyes with someone in your audience if not needed. Additionally, it consumes you and draws your attention away, disconnecting you from your own individual thoughts. Some cases, such as someone presenting a question to you, might require more direct interactions. Otherwise, if you are the only speaker, try to look around without seeing anyone.

Next, consider the volume of your voice. Cadence was discussed extensively, and the recurring idea behind it involved balancing speed; not flying through it too quickly, but also not drawing and drooling out every single syllable. In this same way, the proper balance of vocal volume helps you find a middle ground between whispering and screaming your head off. This can be difficult to determine, but listening to or observing other speeches serves as a good point of reference as to how to balance your volume.

Going along with this, it is said that a good speaker ought to project while speaking to a group. This does not mean scream or yell. Rather, it encourages "throwing your voice" to the back of the room. Speak with vocal inflection, keep your personality in your tone, but speak with a level of determination with your volume as if you are speaking to someone at the opposite end of a long hallway or a large room. This technique is less about the actual volume of your voice and more about vocal tone, so it should be adopted even if you are speaking into a microphone.

Returning to the subject of handling nerves in front of people, there is a common joke about imagining your audience in their underwear, or simply without any clothes at all. Although it is a humorous trope as related to public speaking, even serving as a common joke in cartoons, there are some people who legitimately utilize this technique. Why? Is this some sort of perversion that helps people relax, or is there something else to it? Hopefully, it is the latter.

What word comes to mind when you think of someone being caught in public while in their underwear? Other than "problematic," one word that comes to mind is "exposed." The individual is "exposed" and, as a result "vulnerable." Who else is someone that is exposed and vulnerable? Consider yourself when you are speaking in public! As a speaker, most of your nerves and anxiety come from the audience, or at least the fear of what your audience will think of you if you make a vital mistake. What better way to cope with this mentality than to project that vulnerability being cast onto you right back at them? If this works for you, then consider other options. The audience does not necessarily have to be naked or in their underwear. Try different things. Use your imagination to see the audience as if they were exposed or vulnerable in different ways. What if they were in mismatching clothes, or even just dressed up as clowns?

With these ideas circulating around, it should be noted that you ought not to lose respect and reverence for your audience altogether. These techniques are merely to assist you in the short-term. Overall, you ought to respect your audience and revere their opinion of you, earning it to the best of your abilities. After all, you would not be addressing them in the first place if you were not trying to win them over.

Finally, try to flip the tables and put yourself in the position of an audience member. As such, treat whoever is speaking to you with the same level of respect and attention that you would want if the roles were again reversed. Communicate to whomever is addressing you that you care about what they have to say, what they have to contribute. They have gone out of their way to be here, whether by a little or a lot; and are increasing your knowledge base to some degree, whether by a little or a lot. Thank them by doing the bare minimum: paying attention and acting with reverence and respect.

While the purpose of discussing public speaking within the context of interpersonal communication has been discussed, it is worth noting that these tips and tricks are not only applicable to the specific act of public speaking. Additionally, they do not only have to be applied when speaking in a group setting, either. Rather, they have been worded and phrased very specifically in order to encompass any form of social communication. You may deal with anxiety at the thought of having to network at an event; perhaps you are getting ready to meet your significant other's family for the first time, or perhaps you are just nervous to speak to your waiter or waitress when ordering dinner. No matter where you are in the infinite number of possibilities and circumstances, these tips can be applied to any setting that you need them for. Learn them. Personalize them. Master them.

Chapter 9: Social Gatherings

As we have come to see in Part II, environments play such an enormous role in not only what we communicate, but how we go about it. Furthermore, every little component of how we go about it undoubtedly comes into play. Each chapter thus far has extensively discussed some of the semantics of each particular environment. For the most part, each particular environment was given some specifications that can applied to a whole array of contexts and situations, even different variations of settings within each category. However, the final portion of Part II will discuss an environment that cannot be narrowed down so easily, and it is that of "Social Gatherings."

When you hear this term, what are the first few settings that come to mind? A night on the town bar-hopping with a group of friends? Dinner parties with the boss's family? Obligatory Christmas gatherings with your significant other's side of the family? Getting together with other people could take place at a restaurant, a movie theater, or even simply just another person's home for a simple party. Social gatherings do not have to have a purpose or agenda, nor do they need to have a specific itinerary of things to do.

With this broad spectrum in mind, how can we narrow things down a little bit to where it is not so overwhelming? Breaking the term down to their singular words, "social" and "gathering," gives us a good starting place. We can first specify that "social" ought to refer to interacting with other people. For the sake of this discussion, let us establish and presume that these people being interacted with are outside of your own family. They may include co-workers, new people you recently became acquainted with, or simply your friends. Although you can certainly socialize with your family, the chapter on the home environment went into more detail about family interactions and mutual respect. As a result, this portion will be more friend-centric.

Additionally, it can and should be safely assumed that you are fairly well acquainted with the people you are getting together with. Different sections of Parts I and II both discussed how difficult it can be meeting new people. However, there is likely some level of comfort with people you already know.

Now that we have contextualized the word "social," let us move on to "gathering." This one is simpler and straightforward, though it is not specific by any means. The word can be defined as people coming together to a designated location. Just as family is excluded from this concept, dating scenarios will be left out as well, as it was discussed extensively in Part I. In fact, two people coming together is less of a "social gathering" and more of just an "outing" itself.

There's a common phrase: "read the room." This idea suggests that people determine their actions and statements based around how others are feeling or acting. Essentially, being able to "read the room" is a social skill to develop, just as one has to learn how to start a conversation. Entire portions of this book have been dedicated toward discussing how to interact with people that you are not familiar with; and with exception to public speaking, most of these sections deal with either individual interactions with one other person or small groups of familiar people such as family and friends. Are your interactions going to be different when walking into a house party or a game night with a group of people that you are acquainting yourself with for the first time? How can you read the effect of people that you do not know yet?

Very much like being able to start a new job and figure out your daily attire, soaking in your surroundings and seeing how others are presenting themselves is a good philosophy to take in for thriving in social gatherings. Simply put, look around you. Are people walking around and talking? Are people dancing? Are most others just sitting around and keeping to themselves?

On the subject of attire, if this is a formal event, there is nothing wrong with asking the host about the attire upon being invited. Otherwise, consider who invited you and what the agenda or objective of the gathering is. The key to any gathering is to make yourself both presentable and approachable. Although they were technically in tuxedos for a formal event, you do not want to wind up like Harry & Lloyd in *Dumb and Dumber,* sporting an orange or baby blue tuxedo. While there are times to stand out and express yourself, these are not necessarily such times. If you do have a craving to express yourself and let your personality run wild, consider the remainder of this chapter as an opportunity to let your personality shine when your attire does not or cannot within certain contexts.

Going back to reading the room, and assuming there is no predesignated agenda or activity, consider the overall mood of the people around you. If things are chill and relaxed, it probably would not be best to come bursting into a room with blaring music and start dancing. In this same way, moping in the corner and trying to get people to relax when things are upbeat would be a mood killer. Try to have fun and go with the flow of how the gathering is going already. If this mood is not for you, there is nothing wrong with that. However, it would be better to simply excuse yourself and leave than ruin the mood of those around you.

In that same way, there may be instances where there is an overall mood that is not desirable. Maybe a group gathered to have a good time, but everyone present is moping around, waiting for something to happen. This obviously requires going back to the idea of reading the room. Should you find yourself struggling to assess whether people are in a good mood or not, or if the party needs some life brought to it, sometimes it might be as simple as asking people whether or not they are having a good time. At the very least, doing so breaks the ice and might initiate a conversation with someone new, maybe even with a group of people that you did not know previously.

Another way to read the room is actually to look toward yourself. What kind of a time are you having? Are you enjoying the overall mood, or do you find yourself bored? Perhaps the very reason that you are feeling the need to read the room at all is because you are not having a good time, and you want to see if anyone else is showing signs of feeling the same way. Again, if everyone is having fun and you are not, maybe consider another activity, but this is why it is good to read the room and see if your sentiment is shared.

If others do indeed express to you that they are not enjoying themselves, or they perhaps are a little bored, consider making a suggestion to go do something else. If your town has a night life, suggest going out and doing something as a group. Maybe there is another activity to engage in at the social event. What you decide to suggest is contingent on the event itself and what is already occurring, as well as what is available to do. This is where manners and common decency come into the mix.

Let us take what we have discussed so far and apply it to a hypothetical scenario. Imagine that an acquaintance is throwing a party at his house and about seventy-five people show up. The party does not have a primary objective or group activity, and people are just intermingling as food and drinks are provided. Outside of this, there is very little to do other than sit around and talk. By the time you have arrived, most people have shown up and have found a seat to sit on or lean against. You grab a drink and start to circulate only to find out that you know absolutely no one outside of the host, and even he is someone you are only somewhat familiar with in passing.

As you continue to circulate, you are surprised at how nice your friend's house is. It is very modern, and all the furnishings seem high-end to the point where you find yourself hesitant to even sit down on any furniture in fear of scuffing the fine white finish. However, as you introduce yourself to more and more people, you are underwhelmed at the spirit of the conversations taking place. They are not as lively or engaging as you had hoped coming here. It is almost as if everyone is kind of bored. Though the house is beautiful, it is as sterile as the stereotypical modern house in a magazine. There is literally nothing to do but talk, and no one at the party knows each other. No television or music is playing in the background, and there is almost an uncomfortably low level of volume, despite the quantity of people present. No one has anything but some food and a glass of wine.

Despite this, you find yourself joining a small group of five people that have been sitting around and talking for some time. Although you are enjoying yourself more than before, the life of the party is just not there. Everyone seems to be in agreement, and a passive discussion of what to do about it ensues. All of a sudden, someone in your group points out that the host has a pool in the backyard, and how funny it would be for the group to turn this event into a pool party to liven things up.

Pause the scenario for a moment. What are your thoughts as the reader? Do you agree that it would be fun to throw a twist on things by jumping in the pool? After all, how often do you get to go to a higher end house party? While it would no doubt make things a little crazier, and despite this party being somewhat underwhelming, consider the host. They have clearly put time and money into this party, having the place professionally cleaned and purchasing food and drinks for seventy-five some-odd people. How rude would it be to make even more of a mess to clean up?

Back at the party, you find yourself casually interjecting the suggestion to go downtown for the remainder of the evening. Someone else jumps in and says that they heard about this new rooftop bar that had opened up a few weeks ago, and everyone is in agreement that it would be more fun to check that out. As the others are gathering their things to leave, you find the host and thank him for inviting you and opening his home up. Your group leaves and congregates again at the suggested rooftop bar, and you all end up having a better time for it.

The following morning, you send a quick text to the host of the party to thank him again for inviting you, but you also ask how things ended up going after you had left. They respond, saying that things had been fine up until the point where someone had the bright idea of jumping in the pool that he had just put in the back, and everyone decided to go outside and congregate around. He was the only one left to clean up all of the trash that had accumulated both in and around the new pool.

Think about how you would have felt if you had put all of this work, time, and money into a nice evening all to have someone trash everything. Sure, the party was dull, but you and your new friends ended up making the mature and wise choice of going to do something else. More so, you ended up having a better time because of it. You managed to make four new friends, and you even asked out one of them on a bold whim, so you have a date next Saturday night because of it. Look at how well reading the room worked out for you and your new friends!

Author's Experience

Every year, one side of my family has a Christmas gathering. Despite calling it such, it never takes place on Christmas, and is usually on or after New Year's Day. Frankly, these gatherings have become something to dread. While it is nice to see relatives, there is a mood and feeling associated with these events that is potent yet hard to describe. The best way to summarize them is that they feel obligatory and insincere. Rarely does anyone on this side of the family communicate with one another outside of these events, and the little communication that does occur is usually about planning for this Christmas party.

The oddest thing about all of this is that most of the family lives in the small town. My immediate family lives about an hour away, and my grandparents reside about three hours away, but everyone else lives in the same small town. There is really no excuse for the family to seem so distant, though everyone seems to be content keeping to their own lives.

With all of this context in place, you can imagine how uncomfortable these parties can feel. They are very much treated like a formal event instead of a family gathering, and after not talking for a year, people are asked to awkwardly recall and recite what occurred in the past year when called upon. Many times, the conversation is so sterile, random people are simply called upon to start talking, then that conversation dies out, and the silence returns.

Unlike the scenario discussed in the chapter, these gatherings are not so easily dealt with. When meeting with and being hosted by family, it is not as simple as getting up and leaving if you are bored or uncomfortable. What do you do? Some might suggest you just suck it up and fight through, that doing this once a year is not the end of the world. However, I think I have found a solution that has certainly worked when I have tested it at these events, and may even work for you, should you find yourself in a similar situation.

If a situation feels awkward and stiff, it may be safe to assume that people feel as if they are not themselves. Furthermore, they may even feel as if they are not even able to be themselves, and do not engage in natural and relaxed interactions as a result. While not a guaranteed elixir, perhaps what might work is to introduce the idea of acting natural and being yourself, sending a subliminal message that the world won't end if you were to just relax a little bit and let your guard.

I like using humor to lighten an uncomfortable mood. I have found that this works for my extended family for the most part, as many of them do indeed have a good sense of humor, but tend to suppress it for family gatherings for some inexplicable reason. If and when I am asked a question, I might answer in a silly or sarcastic way to start, then give a genuine answer. I try to keep the humor light and subtle so as not to be obnoxious and never disrespectful or at the expense of others, but it always seems to be just enough to make things feel less heavy.

While this section may seem bloated and excessive for such a small, specific instance and technique, it should be noted that your behavior in public should be very thought out. Yes, be yourself and express yourself, but consider how you are coming across to others. This is not so much suggesting that you have to "fake it 'til you make it" but you certainly do not want to come across as annoying or irritating, as people will remember you as such. Additionally, you do not want to ruin a mood if others are enjoying themselves. This constantly goes back to the idea of "reading the room" to be able to gauge how vested others around you are or are not. It all comes down to making sure you are yourself, but are still considerate of those around you.

As discussed in the "Author's Experience" portion, find your own way of lightening a conversation. Break the ice, and make it feel authentic, natural, and free-flowing. No one likes to be uncomfortable or feel as if they are in an awkward situation. After all, the entire purpose of getting together with others through social gatherings is to interact in a fun and natural way.

Especially within our modern age, there is an unarguable issue with the need for "constant stimulation." The idea is that people have felt the need to be constantly entertained, as we are undoubtedly overexposed to technology and its ready access. While there is no debate that we have been spoiled by having the Internet at our fingertips any time of day or night, do not get this confused with feeling uncomfortable or bored in social situations. If you cannot socialize and enjoy yourself during a social outing, then decide how to take action, even if that means leaving.

Chapter 10:
The Effect of the Cause

Think about your everyday life and all of the mundane activities and tasks that you engage in without so much as a second thought. Brushing your teeth, making a purchase at the store, going to work, watching a television show. These are things that we are practically programmed to do on a daily basis, and it is rare for us to question these natural tendencies within our society.

If you take a moment to break down the reasoning and motivations for the things we do, there is a clear result that we are striving for. The reason for brushing one's teeth is to stay healthy, yes, but also to have clean and white teeth. In making a purchase, we go to a designated location or website and provide the tangible asset of money in order to receive a good. Most of us go to a job almost every day of the week in order to earn income and pursue some relative level of comfort and stability.

All of this is based around a cause and effect model: "I do _____, so that _____." The "cause" is the action that results in the desirable, strived-for "effect." How does this apply to communication? As we have taken a look at several different groups that are typically encountered in society, as well as settings that are also commonly encountered, we have to eventually come to a place where we are questioning whether or not what we are doing is working. We have to be able to objectively look at ourselves and figure out whether we are receiving the desired effect from our many ways of communicating. After all, the truth is that this book is only based on one person's perspectives and experiences. There is no guarantee that what works for some will work for everyone, which is the case for any book or piece of writing. Is there a universal way of knowing whether or not you are an effective communicator?

Even despite my many disclaimers throughout this book that not everything is going to work the same for everyone, and no two people have identical experiences with anything in life, I do wholeheartedly believe that there is a universal idea of knowing whether or not our many efforts and methods of communication are effective. We must confront ourselves with a very simple question: "Am I being understood?"

This goes so far beyond whether or not people physically hear you. It goes beyond whether or not people see your efforts. It goes even further past whether or not others see your efforts and feel as if you are genuine, and your heart is in the right place. Rather, you must question whether or not things are happening as a result of your efforts to communicate. If they are, then you must be doing something right. If things are not happening in the desired or needed way, it is time to take a look under the hood and figure out the problem before moving forward.

For example, there is a model for treatment that is used in addiction recovery. Whether it is drugs, alcohol, or even a dependence on pornographic material, the layout of the model is in a circular pattern. Recovery is not a straight line because it takes "relapse" into account. If relapse occurs, the one struggling is not held in contempt or looked down upon by those caring for them (in the ideal situation, of course). Rather, messing up is literally part of the recovery. You cannot learn to walk without falling a few times. Expecting perfection from anyone, much less someone that is trying to learn and develop, is absurd.

In the same way, do not be too hard on yourself if you are struggling to develop some of the communication skills discussed in this book. Every skill worth learning takes time to develop. At the end of the day, you are striving to make effective communication a natural skill set, so much so that it is not a major thought throughout your day. If you find yourself more timid and reserved, do not fret. In fact, try and embrace who you are. After all, shyness is not a flaw but, rather, a personality trait. It ought not to be treated as a social disability.

You may also be asking yourself what the difference is between a truly effective communicator and someone who just talks a lot; maybe even at a loud, obnoxious tone so that everyone can hear what they have to say. The difference goes back to two principles of this book. Firstly, communication is definitively a back-and-forth process. If information is being put out there by a party, who is on the receiving end of it? Is that information being processed, and is something occurring as a result of it? If we are talking about someone who is loud, obnoxious, and lacks all sense of self-awareness, then the only likely outcome is that people will want to get away from them. That person is HEARD, but not LISTENED TO. On the other end of the spectrum, the information being communicated and conveyed by an effective communicator will be processed, and people listening to them will act accordingly. Whether the actions taken by others are that of simply responding in conversation or engaging in an active, tangible response, an effective communicator will know when people are listening as opposed to simply physically hearing.

In discussing this idea, one prominent example that rings out is that of Paul Revere. If you are not familiar with his story, he was responsible for alerting the town of Lexington, Massachusetts, that the British "red coat" soldiers were coming to invade during the American Revolution. In preparation for any sign of invasion, Paul Revere established a system in which one lantern would be lit in the Old North Church of Lexington if the British were invading on foot, and two would be lit if they were invading by boat. This plan is manifested within the famous quote "One, if by land, and two, if by sea." One night, two lanterns were lit in the steeple, communicating that the British were invading by sea. He alerted the town by taking to a horse (it is unknown whether the horse was his or borrowed) and going on what would later be referred to as "The Midnight Ride." Legend has it that he rode throughout the town, proclaiming "The British are coming! The British are coming!" This is thought to be a fabricated quote. Regardless, the minute men were able to prepare for the invasion as a result of both the system that he established and his subsequent Midnight Ride.

One of the reasons that this story stands out in discussing how to know whether or not you were effective is because of the specific factors at stake. Firstly, it was not Paul Revere's responsibility to win any subsequent battle fought after an invasion. He understood his responsibility: that of alerting the town and the militia to prepare for an invasion. In preparation for doing so, he established a quick, clear, and effective system, which in and of itself was a powerful method of communication. Also consider the follow-through of the town whom he alerted. So often we narrow our perspective to only think of communication as a conversation. Did the townspeople of Lexington stop him and his horse in order to engage in a back-and-forth about the approaching invasion? Absolutely not. Whatever it was that he really said and did that evening, whether it was yelling "The British are coming!" or otherwise, the citizens understood the urgency of the matter and took action. Some speculate that this plan may have been one of the major turning points of the Revolutionary War, in favor of America, all thanks to the quick and effective communication of one Paul Revere.

This book was strategically organized and oriented toward helping the reader compartmentalize all of the different areas in which communication may manifest itself differently. One of the core reasons behind this setup has been to get you thinking about both your strengths and weaknesses. Are you better at communicating to certain groups of people? If so, who? Is communication easier for you within certain contexts, environments, or settings? While it is important for you to become more aware of the areas that need improvement and hone in on those needs, it is equally as important for you to feel good about the areas in which you excel. Think back on a time where your attempts and means of communication were well received, understood, processed, and maybe even appreciated. Who were you communicating with? What was your objective in doing so? Were you trying to pass along good news or bad? Was this an experience that you were looking forward to and anticipating? Where were you when you did this? Comprehend everything about the experience(s), especially your approach, and try to apply it to the areas in which you could use some improvement.

Additionally, this book is not solely meant to tell you how to communicate. It is also meant to get you thinking about any areas of your life where you are a strong and effective communicator and empower you in those fields. After all, by purchasing this book, you communicated to yourself that you have the desire to be a stronger and more effective communicator. Going back to the addiction cycle, the first step in recovery is that of admitting that you have a problem and that you need help. Similarly, whether you are an excellent and experienced communicator, or if the journey to such a state is an uphill climb all the way, you must humble yourself and acknowledge that you still have a lot to learn. Jimi Hendrix, the man that some consider the greatest guitarist of all time, was once asked by Dick Cavett if he agreed that he is indeed the greatest guitar player in the world. Hendrix immediately refuted the claim, and was clearly humbled by it, but insisted that he was merely the best guitarist sitting in his own chair.

While the status of the world's greatest guitarist is undoubtedly a topic amongst musicians and fans alike, there is no doubt that Hendrix is one of the greatest to have taken the stage. He was so prolific in his playing that there is an old legend that many fellow rock guitarists plotted his demise in order to allow for others to have a chance to shine. Regardless, Jimi's humility and modesty is an excellent example to anyone who is looking to master any skill, even communication. Even if you consider one of the best, if not THE best, there is still always room to grow and become better.

Author's Experience

Throughout this book, I have discussed my experiences in the mental health field and the many lessons that I have been fortunate enough to take away from them. One of the most prominent of these lessons is that the ability to communicate is not something to take for granted. Having worked with a very diverse population, I encountered all sorts of different people with different kinds of struggles. The main objective of my work in that position was to meet the clients where they were, both physically and in their life circumstances, and assist them with being able to function and navigate through society.

While every person experiences mental health in their own way, meaning that no two people with the same diagnosis necessarily experience their mutual condition in the same way, there is tremendous diversity in varying levels of independence. Some with diagnoses that are traditionally more extreme found themselves able to carry a job and live in their own space, while others with typically more mild diagnoses were completely dependent and could not live alone. While one has to take into account that the providers of some of these people may have made mistakes when diagnosing, there is still no doubt that this diversity was certainly present and legitimate.

With all of this said, one of the most consistently difficult mental health struggles for people to live with were ones which involved not being able to speak. These are known as "nonverbal" mental health conditions, the most commonly known one being "nonverbal autism." Can you imagine the frustration of growing up, not being able to speak and express yourself? For many, responding with a simple "yes" or "no" for themself is incredibly difficult, as differentiating between the two can be a challenge all its own. Can you also imagine how anxiety-enduring this is for the parents of these children, who are trying to figure out how to help them but have little to no way of knowing what they are in need of? It only becomes more difficult as time goes on and they become older.

Thankfully, we live in an incredible age. There has been a growth in speech and occupational therapy centers that provide children experiencing autism, both verbal and nonverbal, with a friendly and exciting environment to learn the skills needed to develop. Additionally, thanks to the ready access to advanced technology, there are applications designed to help individuals experiencing nonverbal mental health struggles to communicate with those around them. With their phone or tablet, they are able to hit designated buttons that are easy to access, even if they are having anxiety and are struggling to focus.

I wanted to use this opportunity to bring light to a struggle that many experience, which is certainly not addressed to the extent that it ought to be. Although there are great resources coming about, as I had mentioned, there can always be more to help these individuals. Perhaps even consider utilizing the skills in communication that you have been naturally given, and especially considering that you are looking to strengthen them, and advocate for those who are unable to do so for themselves. Consider contacting a community center or mental health practice in your area to see what you can do to volunteer and give a voice to the voiceless.

Conclusion

Unfortunately, our journey together is coming to an end. Although the overarching theme of this book has been that of interpersonal communication, we have had the opportunity to look over so many different components of communication as a whole; different environments, people, contexts, etc. Inevitably, some of these have been more applicable to you than others. However, what is also inevitable is that you have, and will, need to continue to communicate with others in life. No matter how secluded or isolated you or others are, communication will always occur and serve some sort of purpose.

Try and think about some contexts or groups of people that were not discussed during our time together. Although the subject of meeting new friends, going on first dates, and overall family interactions were discussed, would you not consider meeting distant family members for the first time a subject all its own? It is admittedly a little intimidating and daunting to ponder the fact that most of us have extended family members that we have never met and perhaps will never encounter. However, if and when you do encounter them, will it be any different than simply making a new friend? What does your culture promote? What does their culture promote? Will you hug them? Kiss them on the cheek? Shake their hand? Bow? If you eat with them, will there be some form of prayer or ritual to bless the meal? Even the simplest of interactions with a different population can be a lot to ponder, especially considering that these questions are merely scratching the surface.

Another group that would have been fun to discuss is that of meeting the family of a new significant other for the first time. It is a concept that has been addressed in comedies and horror movies alike. Hopefully, the family you are meeting does not resemble the one in Jordan Peele's *Get Out*. In the same way that there are so many questions to consider when meeting new members of your extended family, it is probably best to discuss culture with your significant other prior to encountering them. While being the most authentic form of yourself is important, being respectful and formal is equally important. Think back on the chapter in which workplace behavior and attire were discussed; being professional and formal is not being fake or inauthentic. Rather, it is a form of communication to those around you that their perspective of you is something to be valued and, as a result, you are going out of your way to assure that they approve. How important is it for the family of your significant other to feel that same sense of respect and pride? Do you think they would take comfort in someone that completely disregards their opinion(s) in order to have a good time? Do you think that doing so is planting the seeds of trust in their front yard?

Although some of these types of interactions were discussed within the subjects outlined in the book, one could produce an entire book on electronic communication in and of itself. What do your emails look like? What do your calls sound like? What type of information are you revealing or withdrawing in your text messages? Is your social media appropriate to young or professional eyes and ears? The technology that we own and utilize is not a stand-alone entity:

it is an extension of ourselves. Your profile on Facebook or Instagram has your identity attached to it. As a result, it serves as a means of communication to tell onlookers who you are and what you are all about. Is that a scary statement to you, or do you not care? Do the opinions and perspectives of others not matter to you in the slightest, or are they everything? There is no one universal answer to these questions, and you are no better or worse for how you answer. What is important is that you know how you would answer, and that you can answer these questions with at least some sense of conclusiveness and confidence.

How about writing in general, electronic or not? Do you write much in school or at work? If so, are there any consistent themes in the content of what you are working on? Have you received positive or negative feedback? Neutral or indifferent feedback? If you do not find yourself writing at work or in studying, do you write for fun? If so, what? When asked to speak at an event in front of others or online, a subject that was indeed discussed, do you tend to write your words down, outline them, or do you just improvise? Do you enjoy reading recreationally? If so, do you feel as if the words you are consuming are sinking in? Do you get the sense that you are in tune with the author's intentions? Reading and writing is a fascinating form of communication, and one that people seem to tend to have strong feelings about one way or another. Similarly to the other subjects that would have been fun to explore, these two subjects could fill a book in and of themselves, both collectively and respectively.

The vast majority of this book has placed you as the reader into a point-of-view perspective of someone doing the communicating. At any point, did you ever picture yourself as the one receiving the communication? In your mind, did you ever imagine yourself as the boss, another family member, another friend, a co-worker, or even the other party on a date? If so, what was it like? Did you feel as if you were being effectively communicated with, or were you only communicated to?

If on the receiving end of the communication, think about whether or not the one communicating was effective. What did it sound like? Was it something that you would have said or done if in their position? Additionally, use your imagination to think about what emotions may have been experienced on the part of the one receiving the communication. Was a boss sympathetic to the meager employee asking for a raise? Did you accept the pleas of forgiveness from the child caught with their hand in the cookie jar? Could any of these situations have produced different outcomes as a result of better or worse communication methods?

In reality, this concept is one of the primary goals and objectives of this entire book: to help you get to know yourself well enough to be able to answer every single question presented. As your eyes have scanned over these words, and when multiple questions were being posed, were you able to say "yes" or "no" appropriately? Did you feel a sense of certainty if you did? As stated, the answers to the questions presented in this book do not have a concrete answer that is universally applicable. Unlike a sudoku or crossword puzzle book, you cannot jump to the back and peek at the solutions for each inquiry. This is because there is no wrong answer. There is far too much diversity in our world, even within just one small area of land, for everyone to be able to answer a question the same across the board. People vary in size, shape, occupation, social status, wealth, culture, race, ethnicity, sexual orientation, physical appearance, emotional health, mental health, and even taste in music.

For instance, although there is a social notion of "universal truths" and values that some would insist are undebatable, and that 100% of humans would agree on, such as the idea that murdering is wrong, there will always be people with poor mental health or executive functioning that are able and willing to kill an innocent person and perhaps even derive a sense of enjoyment from doing so. Likely, some others might agree with this value, but be willing to commit a murder in order to earn some money. Still others would insist that killing with an objective, such as to prevent something undesirable from happening, or "to prevent more people from getting hurt" if the victim committed crimes of their own would be an acceptable exception to the "universal truth." Capital punishment has always been a hot topic in politics and continues to be to this day. Wars, where murder is an inevitable reality, are also debated. With all this in mind, while most of us can agree that killing or murdering is wrong, hopefully you can see how subjective and complex situations can be.

Although the above can be seen as an extreme example, hopefully it shed some light on the importance of knowing where you stand and how to answer questions about yourself. Being certain about who you are and what you believe is a guaranteed way to ensure a bolder sense of confidence to emit when you encounter others and engage in your own forms of communication, no matter where it is or who you are engaging with.

A recurring theme and disclaimer throughout the whole book has been that of non-universal application. Not everything in here applies to every single reader. While many of the scenarios are relatable to some, others might read them and not know how to apply it to their own lives. Not only are people diverse, but life experiences are as well, and there is no way to write in such a way that every single person can relate to. However, there are key components that are universally applicable; such as the need for friends, the need for a job, the need to interact with family members, and other important needs. If one component is less applicable to you, or if no settings or groups of people were applicable to you along the way, try to take the basics of what was discussed and apply it to your other interactions.

For instance, many people opt to interact with peers through video games online. Although it is a very competitive and often hostile environment, this may just be the more opportunistic choice to socialize for someone that struggles with in-person interactions. Having a familiar, comfortable, and safe space to have fun is going to be more appealing to some than going out, and that is okay. The reality is that this very book was written during a worldwide pandemic, resulting in billions of people becoming isolated from the world. Suddenly, online interactions did not seem so unappealing, as it was virtually the only choice for anyone who had access to the Internet.

The last chapter prior to this conclusion posed the question to you as the reader: "now what?" How do you know whether or not your communication is effective? The general idea of the proposed answer to this is contingent on whether or not the communicator is being heard, and whether or not the information being communicated is receiving some kind of validation, acknowledgement, or even reciprocation. With that proposition, there is another question that I would like to have serve as the ending point of this book: "what is the most important kind of communication that we can engage in?" Some might cite love as the most important, others might suggest that sending out "good vibes" back into the world is most valuable, and still others might point back toward their own worldview and the communication of it as the absolute truth to be revered.

Very much like a worldview, the value of communication is going to differ from person-to-person. The only absolute of communication is that it is "absolutely subjective." With that said, I would suggest that the most important form of communication is to assure the value of those you care about, and those who care most about you, expelling any room for doubt. Never saying "I love you" to someone you truly do love is one of the universe's truest tragedies. Think about the vastness of communication of which this book merely grazed the surface layer. Do more than just tell your loved ones how you feel. Do you believe the old proverb that "actions speak louder than words?" If not, then come to a place where you do believe it, because it is absolutely true. The ideas of "telling someone" and "showing someone" ought not to even be in the same sentence, as they are nothing alike.

Additionally, communicate to the world by going the extra mile. Harness your abilities and talents; because believe it or not, but you have a set of skills that make you unique from anyone else. Whether or not you have discovered what these abilities are is another conversation entirely. In fact, most of us probably have abilities that we will never discover within

145

our respective lifetimes. Find those talents, make them your own, and do not let others define you. Live a life where your destiny is communicated in past, present, and future tense simultaneously.

At the end of the day, when all is said and done, communication is a tool that is to be used. However subjectively it is utilized, or to whatever extent one runs with it, we all must communicate. Make the most of it. Do not waste it. Regardless of your worldview and belief system, we only have one shot at the life we have been given on this Earth, in these bodies, and with these minds. The voice that each of us has been given differs from anyone that exists now, in the past, or in the future. Use that voice to communicate to the world around you that you are making the most of it.

www.ingramcontent.com/pod-product-compliance
Lightning Source LLC
Chambersburg PA
CBHW071700210326
41597CB00017B/2266